I0051794

The Management Map II...
Navigation Tools for Managers
Transitioning to Leadership

Deborah Avrin, MS, SPHR

ManageSmart Publishing

This publication contains the opinions and ideas of the author. The author and publisher specifically disclaim all responsibility for any liability, loss, or risk, personal or otherwise, that is incurred as a consequence, directly or indirectly, of the uses and applications of this book. Any and all implied or expressed warranties of fitness are hereby disclaimed.

Copyright 2015, 2018 Deborah Avrin
All rights reserved. No part of this book may be reproduced, stored in a retrieval system, or transmitted by any means, electronic, mechanical, photocopying, recording, or otherwise, without written permission from the author.

Published by ManageSmart Publishing
Plano, Texas
972-881-5282

Printed in the United States of America

ISBN: 978-0-9820901-2-1
Cover design: MC2 Graphics

To Sharon Kenerson, my sister, friend, and teacher extraordinaire.

CONTENTS

ACKNOWLEDGMENTS

I am so very grateful for the support I received from family and friends in writing this book.

I would first like to acknowledge Carol Glynn, my book accountability buddy, who is also writing a book. Carol and I would meet for a long lunch every couple weeks to report progress and brainstorm ideas for each of our books. There were so many times I pushed myself to write knowing that it was "book buddy" week and I wanted to be able to report progress. Carol's book, *The Art of Technical Training Tools, Techniques, and Tales* is going to be wonderful and much needed in the marketplace.

A big thank you also goes out to my content team of experts who agreed to be forthright in their feedback and use the supplied red pen on an almost final draft of the book. I can honestly say it is a much better book as a result of the contributions of Sara Belmontes, Julie Chance, Dee Dick, Amy Hardin, Amber James, Judy Martin, and Sherrie Tarpley.

I am grateful to have worked with an amazing group of experts in making the book professional both inside and out; Alan McCuller who designed the cover to match the first book and my two editors, Judy Hoffman and Martha McCuller, who patiently corrected my grammar and punctuation. Don't blame the editors if I went "rogue" and didn't listen to them.

Finally, a thank you goes out to my husband, Stuart Avrin, who put up with my stressing over the writing of this book. I promised him it was the last one but he doesn't believe me!

INTRODUCTION

Since writing *The Management Map...Navigation Tools for the New Manager*, I've frequently received the question, "When are you going to write another book?"

I protested for years that I wasn't going to write another book and that *The Management Map* would be an only child. However, one day instead of my usual "no way" response I paused, reflected, and asked the question, "If I were to write another book, what would it contain?" As what usually happens when you change your mindset, a new insight appears.

The new insight led me to write this book specifically for experienced managers. *The Management Map II... Navigation Tools for the Experienced Manager* delves deeper into many of the concepts introduced in the first book plus many new topics. Reading the first book, which I'll refer to throughout this book as *The Management Map (TMM)*, is recommended but not necessary before reading this one. As with the first book, I use a management map as a metaphor for creating a resource of knowledge you can draw from during your journey as a manager. The more diverse experiences you have, the larger your map.

Each chapter contains a wealth of practical tips I have learned during a career in human resources and in developing and delivering management programs to a wide client base. At the end of each chapter is a list of follow-up activities and training topics to help you continue to build your own management map.

Even though you may have many years in management, when you change your mindset from the way you've been doing things to trying some of the new concepts in *The Management Map II*, you may gain new insight. Enjoy the journey!

(Yes...this is the very last book!)

ONE

ON THE ROAD AGAIN...
Advanced Management Mapping

Chapter Learning Points
- Challenges and skills of an experienced manager
- Begin the transition to leadership

> *"On the road again / Goin' places that I've never been / Seein' things that I may never see again / And I can't wait to get on the road again."*
>
> ~Willie Nelson, songwriter

> *"People grow through experience if they meet life honestly and courageously. This is how character is built."*
>
> ~Eleanor Roosevelt, longest-serving First Lady of the United States

Reflection of an Experienced Manager

A celebration is going on outside of Judy's office. Michael has just been promoted to his first management position, and his many well-wishers have brought a cake and cards.

Judy reflects on her first years as a manager and knows that Michael has a lot to learn about management after the excitement about the new job wears off. Judy's first few years as a manager were challenging, and she "stubbed her toe" a few times. Luckily she had a great role model in her manager, Linda, and attended the management development classes her company offered. Judy has gained experience and confidence but also realizes there is always more to learn about being a manager.

Judy gets up to join the party to congratulate Michael on starting his management journey and to offer her experience to assist him along the way. She laughs that Michael won't understand when she tells him about developing his management map, but she knows that eventually he will see the benefits when he navigates during his management journey!

You've Gained Experience as a Manager…Now What?

You've gained experience and confidence as a manager, so it's time to dust off your management vision and update your management map with new and updated navigation skills. You realize you've been looking at just a corner of your management map, and as you start unfolding and opening more and more of your map you see the potential for growth unfolding before you.

As you began your management journey, you visualized the type of manager you wanted to become. You created your vision by thinking of your most important values, your strengths, and what you will regret not doing or achieving when you retire from your management career.

Having been in management for a while, you realize that your original vision might not be practical or you have strayed off the original path you established for yourself. Many managers have seen the benefit of completing the vision activity from *TMM* after they have been in their job a few years. Let's get on the road again and explore what it's like for an experienced manager.

> *"Nothing ever becomes real till it is experienced."*
>
> ~John Keats, English poet

Every business and position has a yearly cycle. During the first year as a manager, you were learning, and probably making a few mistakes along the way. Every quarter probably brought another new challenge. In the second year on the job, new managers can now anticipate what will be required for each quarter and perfect their performance, remembering the mistakes from last year. It's probably not until year three as a manager that they are comfortable enough to breathe, reflect, and are ready to build new skills. But guess what? Every time you get a new team to manage or start with a new company, the cycle starts over. Experienced managers are ready to meet the challenges based on what they learned in prior positions.

In *TMM* we discussed the three C's: confidence, competence, and courage. As an experienced manager you can probably relate to numerous situations where you have needed all three C's. Here are several differences between being a new manager and an experienced manager.

New Managers vs. Experienced Managers

New Manager	Experienced Manager
• Every situation is new	• Competence developed from management experiences over time
• Verify decisions with others	• Confidence in decision making; you've had past successes and have learned "what works"
• Reluctance to delegate	• Courage to delegate; you've overcome the "do it myself" trap
• Following standards step-by-step	• Courage to challenge the status quo

When you were promoted to your first managerial position, you probably supervised a small group of employees in entry-level positions. As an experienced manager, you may be supervising professional employees and have a larger team requiring another layer, such as a team lead or supervisor.

As a new manager, you focused on the day-to-day of managing your team as you learned the skills needed to manage effectively. Your concern was the immediate productivity and quality of the results of your team. As an experienced manager, you now reach out beyond your own team and see how it fits into the larger picture of your company as a whole and within the industry in which your company does business.

In the chapter "Visualizing Your Management Map" in *TMM*, we learned about four traps many new managers experience. The four traps are: Carrot and Stick, Apologetic, Buddy and Pal, and Do-it-Myself. Traps that experienced managers may experience include:

- **Lone Wolf** – This trap has managers thinking, "They gave me this promotion, so I should be the one to make all the decisions" or "It will be too difficult to gain consensus from everyone, so I'll just make the decision." By failing to seek out the opinions of others before making decisions, you are cutting yourself off from alternative perspectives and the sense of involvement and commitment your team members would feel by participating. Remember, participation equals engagement.

- **Missing in Action** – This trap occurs when your team members have trouble getting "face time" with you because you're frequently unavailable to them. As you gain experience, your time will be in high demand with all the meetings you attend as well as increased membership on project teams and task forces. You may be tempted to hide behind closed doors as you work on follow-up items and complete required regular reports. Not being available to your team will result in major consequences. The most important consequence is giving the perception you can't be approached with a concern or question. If you aren't available for team members when they have a question, they will do one of three things: 1) ask someone else, who may or may not know the correct answer, 2) figure it out themselves, which may or may not be correct, or 3) do nothing until you are available. None of these options would be considered acceptable.

- **Fear of Skill Obsolescence** – Many managers are promoted based on their technical skills in their department, and the longer they spend in management the more they start to realize they can no longer do some of the tasks the members of their team are doing. Fear starts to creep in with the realization of no longer being the best "technical expert" in the group. This drives some managers to start taking on tasks that should be completed by their team members, falling back into the "do it myself" trap. Time to let go! Your job is to help your team members be the best they can be so they can truly own their jobs. If you do their jobs, you won't have time for your managerial duties.

- **Interpersonally Unaware** – This trap has to do with being unaware of how your behavior and comments impact others. Does your tone of voice keep people from approaching you, creating an atmosphere where employees don't feel they can talk to you or question your ideas? Do you think you're funny but your humor is actually offensive to others? Can you sense when your team members are bothered about something but are not speaking up? Experienced managers hone their empathy skills to be able to sense other people's emotions and "put themselves in the shoes" of how others might feel or perceive a situation. Managers need empathy to develop a high degree of trust and communication with their team members. Without empathy, managers may leave "collateral damage" in their wake without even realizing it.

> *"If your emotional abilities aren't in hand, if you don't have self-awareness, if you are not able to manage your distressing emotions, if you can't have empathy and have effective relationships, then no matter how smart you are, you are not going to get very far."*
>
> ~Daniel Goleman, psychologist and author

Skills of an Experienced Manager

What skills and abilities should an experienced manager have? Review the checklist below as you think about your competency in each area.

- Thinking strategically and participating in higher-level decision making in your organization
- Expanding your perspective outside your department into other areas of your company and industry
- Comprehending and managing the organizational culture of your department
- Hiring talented, highly engaged team members who fit within your culture
- Challenging employees to grow in their abilities and careers by providing encouragement and direction
- Creating an environment where employees feel engaged and participatory
- Having the courage to confront the challenging people-type situations and avoiding the price of delay

In the upcoming chapters you will gain insight and skills to develop each of the competencies listed.

Transitioning from Manager to Leader

Once experienced managers feel comfortable with their responsibilities, they begin to develop their leadership skills. Management and leadership skills are linked and complementary. Leadership can be defined as a one-to-many relationship, as opposed to the one-to-one relationship of management.

> *"The work that leaders do—the work that really matters—is boiled down to three areas: crafting a vision, building alignment, and championing execution. Vision, Alignment, and Execution are 'magic words.' They strike a chord that turns the goal of leadership into tangible steps."*
>
> *~The Work of Leaders*

What are some of the most important things managers could be doing right now to prepare for developing their leadership skills? Here a few ideas to consider:

- **Crafting a Vision** – Leaders at every level need to have a vision that supports the organization's vision. They need to connect the organization's vision to their team so they can relate how the vision impacts their division, department, function, shift, etc.

- **Aligning the Team** – Leaders need to engage both the head and heart of the team to align them toward the big picture vision. Engaged employees who know where they are going will keep focused and take the initiative to adjust their priorities to accomplish the vision.

- **Having an Expanded Focus** – Leaders should periodically step away from looking within their own organization, division, or department and outwardly scan the external environment for changes that could positively or negatively impact results.

It All Starts With Vision

Vision harnesses the power of imagination to inspire the workforce to look outward toward what the company wants to be in the future. A vision allows the organization or team to create something of unquestionable value, serves customers in an unparalleled fashion, or reinvents the way it does business. In order for vision to be an effective leadership tool, it must accomplish two things simultaneously: 1) it must align your organization and 2) it must promote change.

Consider this impactful, vision statement by President John F. Kennedy that made everyone believe the impossible was possible and launched the space race. "This nation should dedicate itself to achieving the goal, before this decade is out, of landing man on the moon and returning safely to earth."

What do successful visions have in common? They are inspirational, transformational, revolutionary, ambitious, clear, bold, and confident. They make you want to be part of the effort that will achieve the vision. How do they compare to your company's vision?

While the CEO may be responsible for the overall vision, each leader within the organization needs to define a vision for their group that supports the main vision. For example, consider the San Diego Zoo's vision: "To become a world leader at connecting people to wildlife and conservation." The food and beverage manager may be inspired by this vision and develop menu items and packaging that includes facts about wildlife. The marketing manager may include information on the zoo's efforts in wildlife conservation in their advertisements.

It takes leaders at all levels to craft a vision of new possibilities of the future for the company to become what it wants to be. When leaders are focused on how their department contributes to the overall vision, something exciting happens in an organization. The vision becomes the reality, and every member of the company becomes engaged and feels a sense of accomplishment.

Execution after Vision

We've all met leaders who can create an inspired vision for the future of their organizations. Many are charismatic individuals who can inspire others and brilliantly paint a mental picture of how the future will look and feel. The big question is can they make the vision a reality? The answer is execution, which makes the inspirational vision actionable.

> **"Vision without execution is hallucination."**
>
> ~Thomas Edison, inventor

Execution is more than a process, it's the insight and passion that an effective leader can contribute. Leaders don't necessarily need to create the execution plan themselves, but they should always create an environment that leads to more effective execution. Here are a few areas where a leader can make an impact on execution:

- **Ensure People Have Enough Structure** – Part of a leader's job is to ensure that people have what they need to do their work effectively. For many people, not having a well-defined structure for execution will make them nervous. It is important to involve others in the planning process to gain their buy-in and tap into their technical knowledge. Well thought-out plans will include problem solving to eliminate barriers to successful implementation.

- **Have an Infectious Drive** – Leaders set an example on execution momentum by instilling a sense of the possible. It is easy for inertia to set in where actions focus on maintaining the status quo rather than the behavior changes required for the new vision. After the initial introduction of the vision, it is important to get things started immediately by creating a sense of urgency and obtaining commitment to specific deadlines. Leaders can create a culture with a focus on results that propel the development of concrete strategies.

- **Stay Plugged Into the Process** – Leaders keep their fingers on the pulse of the organization, making sure their vision retains the required momentum through execution. By keeping up to date, milestones can be celebrated and corrections can be made if things are off track. Leaders must be willing to praise and also address problems respectfully and quickly to retain momentum.

> *"Leadership is the capacity to translate vision into reality."*
>
> ~Warren Bennis, organizational consultant and author

It takes committed leadership to translate vision into reality. Leaders champion execution by having strategies, committed people, and a results-oriented culture in place.

Summary

As a new manager you learned to effectively use the three C's—competence, confidence, and courage—when you created your management map. Now as an experienced manager you have become aware of new traps to avoid and additional competencies to develop. As your management skills grow, it becomes time to start to grow your leadership skills as well, including developing a vision that will inspire your team.

Building Your Map
Follow-up Activities

1. **Update your management vision.** Review your management vision from the activity in *TMM*. Does it still describe the manager you want to be or does it need an update? Record your final version here and also put it in prominent place to remind you on a regular basis.

   _____

   _____

   _____

2. **Describe how have you used the three C's (competence, confidence, and courage) as an experienced manager.**

   _____

   _____

   _____

3. **Consider the following traps.** Identify if you fall into any of these and take steps to steer away from the trap.
   - ❏ Lone Wolf
   - ❏ Missing in Action
   - ❏ Fear of Skill Obsolescence
   - ❏ Interpersonally Unaware

4. **Assess your competency on the following experienced managerial skill areas on a scale of**

1 = proficient, 2 = acceptable, and 3 = needs development:

(   ) Think strategically and participate in higher-level decision making in your organization

(   ) Expand your perspective outside of your department into your company and industry

(   ) Comprehend and manage the organizational culture of your department

(   ) Hire talented, highly engaged team members who fit within your culture

(   ) Challenge employees to grow in their abilities and careers by providing encouragement and direction

(   ) Create an environment where employees feel engaged and participatory

(   ) Have the courage to confront challenging people situations and avoid the price of delay

5. **List your organization's vision.**

_____

_____

Now list a vision for your team of employees that will inspire their commitment to the organization.

_____

_____

_____

6. **Take the style assessment _Everything DiSC®_ _Work of Leaders_. Create a plan based on the feedback you receive.**

Where to Go From Here
Helpful Training Topics

❑ Visioning skills

❑ Everything DiSC® Work of Leaders

❑ Goal setting

TWO

NAVIGATE GLOBALLY
Understanding the External Marketplace

Chapter Learning Points
- Shift to a global viewpoint
- Think strategically

> *"Think global, act local."*
>
> ~Patrick Geddes, social activist

Think Globally

Christopher Columbus didn't realize when he took out his sextant and began his voyage from Spain to the new world he would be the first to navigate globally. Talk about having courage in the face of the unknown! Before this journey, European voyages had followed coastlines or to previously known lands. Only Columbus had the courage to set off across a broad, unknown sea with no specific previous knowledge of what lay on the other side. He was hoping for Asia, but instead he found another land with great value.

Since Columbus' time the world seems to be getting smaller and smaller. Advances in transportation and technology make it possible for people from different nations, cultures, languages, and backgrounds to communicate, meet, and do business with one another more than ever. British-based Rolls-Royce makes engine parts in Virginia and ships them to Europe and Asia to be assembled in jet engine factories. Siemens, a German company, makes powerplant turbines in North Carolina, most of which are shipped to Saudi Arabia and Mexico.

What if you don't work for an international company? Does this chapter pertain to you? The simple answer is yes, and if your company isn't impacted by global commerce now, it will be in the future. With advancements in e-commerce, even small businesses have the ability to conduct international transactions over the Internet. Even if your customers are not worldwide, some of your suppliers of raw materials likely are global.

Look around at the items you use every day. For example, my computer is from a South Korean company; my mobile phone is from a company in Finland. But both of these companies manufacture their products all over the world and don't restrict themselves to their home country.

Thinking globally also means understanding the environmental connection we have with our world neighbors. Weather and other environmental issues around the globe have the ability to impact us and our companies. A freeze in the Florida citrus orchards reduces the supply of oranges and increases prices for suppliers in other locations. Colder winters in the Northeast increases the demand for fuel oil. A volcanic eruption in Iceland caused the closure of airspace over many European countries, affecting the travel arrangements of hundreds of thousands of people. When a devastating flood in Thailand occurred, it disrupted manufacturing of Japanese technology companies based in Thailand, resulting in a global shortage of hard-disk drives.

Shifting Our View of the World

Take a look at Saul Steinberg's famous 1976 New Yorker cover, *View of the World from 9th Avenue*. The illustration depicts the island of Manhattan, New York, enlarged in the foreground and the rest of the world presented much smaller toward the background. It humorously depicts a New Yorkers' self-image of Manhattan as the center of the world. I wonder if Columbus had a similar picture in his mind with Europe as the center of the world?

It takes courage to look beyond our boundaries and put your company, city, industry, and country in the proper perspective. Global citizens make decisions differently. We can choose to put up barriers to keep foreign competition out or create doors to increase opportunities for global trade.

Globalization allows us to share ideas across nations. New ideas come in the form of products, technological innovations, business models, and all other aspects of business. Globalization has provided many different avenues for companies to acquire raw materials or wholesale products they can sell at a retail level. With globalization, small businesses can choose from many more wholesalers for products to use in their businesses.

In addition to purchasing products or materials from overseas, smaller businesses may also outsource whole functions to these countries. A lot of small businesses do not have the means to create in-house departments for all of their functions such as computer software, marketing, etc. They may outsource these functions to other countries at reasonable prices.

When managers shift their view of the world they are expanding their knowledge and accomplishing several things, including:

- Applying their management practices to be able to virtually manage team members across the country or across the globe
- Valuing diversity, including diversity of thought and experience
- Developing and monitoring for cultural sensitivity
- Practicing strategic thinking, looking past their own boundaries
- Scanning the external environment to connect better with their organization's strategy, customers, and suppliers
- Analyzing strengths, weaknesses, opportunities, and threats (SWOT)

Long Distance Management

As most experienced managers have learned, management can be a challenging job and managing long distance adds another layer of complexity. After starting a company in one location, growth may lead it to expand the business across the US or even globally. With this expansion of business and the advances in technology making working remotely possible, managers will likely become virtual managers now or in the future. A manager in Dallas may have team members located in Salt Lake City, Cincinnati, and Charleston, South Carolina. Another manager may have team members in the US, Europe, and Asia.

The good news is that you can use your knowledge of management and apply it to your expanding "management map" reference. Start by considering the perspective of your virtual employee and then applying a little creativity using technology and other methods available to you.

When managers hear they will be managing virtually, their immediate concerns include communication challenges and measurement of the work. When employees hear they will report to a virtual manager, they also have concerns about feeling "out of the loop" and not being part of day-to-day decision making. Employees who are located offsite sometimes feel that a lack of "face time" during meetings with higher-level executives may hurt their career.

Long distance or virtual management will be addressed in our upcoming chapters; in the meantime here are a few ideas to consider immediately:

- Determine the communication vehicles currently available in your organization. What information or technology do you need to be able to make teleconference or video conference calls?

- Make a list of time zones (a map perhaps) for all your virtual team members so you can establish meeting times that will accommodate everyone's normal working hours if possible.

- Set specific times during the week that you will have a virtual meeting. Don't get into the bad habit of not holding your meetings. If you need to cancel your meeting for an emergency, immediately reschedule.

- Create a place, perhaps with a shared drive on your company's intranet, for everyone to add agenda items for your weekly meeting. Topics can be added anytime you have a thought, such as "I have to remember to tell Sherrie about...." Don't rely on just your memory.

- Include your virtual team members on project teams so they become part of the decision-making process and teach the rest of your team members how to interact virtually.

- If your team members are based in other countries, begin to educate yourself on the culture and customs of each of their countries.

Valuing Diversity

Not all good practices were born in one civilization. The world that we live in today is a result of many cultures coming together.

Why value diversity? The population is changing; our applicants as well as our customers are becoming more diverse. Managers face increased competition to hire the best employees, and those companies that embrace diversity will have a larger pool from which to choose the best and brightest. Basically when managers bring diversity of ideas and experiences together, they achieve a better result because the situation can be examined from many different points of view.

> *"Diversity is about valuing and empowering a healthy mix of employees, recognizing that everyone has something to contribute. It's also about engagement, with employees feeling involved and free to express their ideas. A diverse culture cultivates a climate of mutual respect. Lively conversation is encouraged, often resulting in more creative approaches being put on the table."*
>
> ~Gary Finney, The Dallas Morning News *Texas Diversity* magazine

Having people of diverse cultures, genders, and ages working closely together impacts teamwork. Today, many teams include four unique generations of people in the workplace. Different experiences bring richness to perspectives and decision making. People from each cultural group will contribute more to the team if they feel respected in the workplace. People can't feel like part of the team if they are ignored and not valued.

When my ancestors migrated from Europe to America, the term used was "melting pot." Immigrants were encouraged to melt their nationalities, cultures, and ethnicities together in one big "stew." The current thinking is that people should embrace the beauty of what makes us diverse as we combine our uniqueness with others as a mosaic. If you look closely at a mosaic you can see individual tiles, but placed together in the right way they can create an amazing design. Another metaphor is to look at a flower, individually lovely but when put in an arrangement with other flowers of different color and variety, it becomes something more. Human nature focuses on differences but if we start by looking for commonalities and building trust, we can then openly discuss differences in a respectful way. We can create mosaics and bouquets in our organization.

> *"The world we live is far too competitive to pass up available resources. You'll not win races for long, firing only half of the cylinders in your engine. In my opinion, the only way to be competitive is to use all of the talent you can muster, no matter how it is packaged."*
>
> ~Jack MacAllister, chairman of U.S. West

Cultural Sensitivity

Cultural sensitivity is the awareness and sensitivity of other practices and cultures. Cultural sensitivity skills can include understanding different cultures, how individuals should be properly approached, and how to communicate accordingly. The term cultural sensitivity embodies the knowledge, understanding, skills, and protocols that allow an individual or system to provide services across cultural lines in the best way.

Cultural sensitivity skills are important for your employees to function cohesively as a team that is respectful and courteous to each other regardless of cultural differences. These skills may be especially important for certain employees who regularly interact with outside business clients, many of whom may have diverse backgrounds and heritages. Typically, these skills may include an ability to at least build a functioning professional relationship with others, communicate in a respectful and polite manner according to which culture you are conversing with, and an ability to overlook cultural boundaries and interact on a regular basis for the good of the company.

> *"Tolerance, intercultural dialogue, and respect for diversity are more essential than ever in a world where peoples are becoming more and more closely interconnected."*
>
> ~Kofi Annan, former secretary-general of the United Nations

Experienced managers have a well-developed sense of cultural sensitivity. These managers regularly monitor their work area to ensure everyone on the team feels respected and has the opportunity to make a contribution. Consider the following cultural sensitivity situations when monitoring the work area:

1. Have some of your team members created "cliques" where others are excluded?
2. Are ideas solicited from all team members and not just the very vocal?
3. Do some team members appear to be isolated from the group?
4. Do you regularly consider dietary restrictions and preferences when ordering in lunch or other treats?
5. Do employees feel pressured to participate in holiday and birthday celebrations?

6. Is recognition customized to fit the desires of each team member? For example, some team members are uncomfortable with public recognition.
7. Have words, phrases, and jokes entered into the vocabulary of your department that might be offensive to others?

Be a Lighthouse for Your Organization—Strategic Thinking

Strategic thinking helps managers look out the door to the world and see how it impacts their organizations.

Experienced managers engage in strategic thinking. This type of thinking is sometimes referred to as "big picture" thinking. To use a metaphor, strategic thinking is more like a lighthouse and not a flashlight. The rotational light in a lighthouse scans over the surface of the water and shoreline to aid in waterway navigation and marking hazardous conditions such as a rocky coastline.

"Traditional thinking is all about 'what is.' Future thinking will also need to be about 'what can be.'"

~Edward de Bono, author, inventor, and consultant

How do managers act like a lighthouse, scanning their environment for hazards and opportunities? They collect information and synthesize it to determine if it is critical to the current and future of their organization. Managers can obtain this information by subscribing to publications related to their industry, reading blogs, attending trade association conferences, etc.

Tactical executors carry out initiatives; however, strategic professionals present decision makers with strategic ideas that benefit the entire company. Strategic thinkers are able to strategize effectively at a level that is beneficial to the overall organization. They are able to answer the question: "How do I best address organizational priorities that stretch beyond what matters solely to me?"

Environmental Scanning

One of the best processes to gather intelligence, survey, and interpret data to help anticipate the conditions impacting your industry is a method called environment scan.

Many people use the acronym PEST as a memory aid in their environment scanning analysis. PEST stands for political, economic, social, and technological. If you add two more factors—the environmental and legal factors—the acronym becomes PESTEL.

Managers should examine each factor individually in the context of its impact to their organization and industry.

- **Political** factors include which political party is in office and its views on health, education, infrastructure, and taxes. Major elections in the near future may change the conditions for your industry depending on which party wins the election and its agenda. Companies in large industries will sometimes contribute funds to Political Action Committees (PACs), organized for the purpose of raising and spending money to elect candidates that support their industries' interests and defeat candidates that don't.

- **Economic** factors have a major impact on how businesses operate and make decisions, such as whether the business can grow and the price of exporting and importing goods and raw materials. These factors include economic growth, interest rates, and inflation rates. Some organizations will invite economists to their environmental scanning meeting for their expertise in this area.

- **Social** trends affect the demand for a company's products and how that company operates based on trends in society. Factors include fashion, food, music, and use of technology. Two examples of trends include the current trend away from foods with high carbohydrate content and social media trends.

- **Technological** factors include technological advances in the way we use equipment, automation, and software. Technological shifts can affect cost, quality, and productivity. Technology created in one industry can sometimes be creatively used in others.

- **Environmental** factors include aspects such as weather, climate change, and natural disasters such as hurricanes, tornados, and earthquakes. Your industry and geographic location should be considered in looking at the environment.

- **Legal** factors include existing laws and new legislation. The type of laws that most impact business are employment, antitrust, health and safety, and environmental. Some industries are more highly regulated than others.

Synthesize Information

After your scanning activity, it is important to make the connection with what you just learned by synthesizing. When you synthesize you are taking the new ideas and comparing them to what you already know or do. When strategic thinkers encounter new information they think about:

1. How will this information impact my company in the future?
2. What best practice can I take away and implement from this new information?

After you obtain the information from your PESTEL analysis, you are ready to go on to the next step in the synthesizing process: connecting the data to your organizational strategy, customers, and suppliers.

- **Connect to Organizational Strategy** – How is this information connected to the work you do and the products and services your company provides? Could it change the way you do business now or in the future?

- **Connect to Customers** – What impact to your customers does this information reveal or does it possibly open other sources of customers for your organization?

- **Connect to Suppliers** – What does the information reveal about the possibilities of shortage of raw materials your organization needs? Are there new suppliers in the marketplace?

SWOT Analysis

SWOT is an acronym that stands for strengths, weaknesses, opportunities, and threats. A SWOT analysis is a planning method that assists organizations in developing strategies for implementing their goals. It provides a way to determine the risks and rewards of business decisions.

A SWOT analysis is typically conducted by managers after completing an environment scan. The environmental scan provides managers with information for two pieces of a SWOT analysis: the opportunities and threats that are external to your organization. Strengths and weaknesses are internal factors. You can use a SWOT analysis for your organization, department, product, or even yourself.

Questions to consider in developing your SWOT:
Strengths
- What are our advantages?
- What do other people see as our strengths?
- What is something that our customers value that our competition doesn't have or do?

Weaknesses
- What could we improve?
- What does our competition do better?
- What do our customers complain about?

Opportunities
- What are the external trends that are related to our business?
- What does the market need that we could provide?

- How are we positioned to take advantage of current and future trends?

Threats
- What obstacles do we face?
- What new trends could make us obsolete?
- Is our competition better equipped to meet changes in the marketplace?

You can conduct a more thorough analysis by combining pieces of SWOT:

- **S-O analysis (strengths-opportunities)** – How can our strengths be employed to take advantage of development opportunities?

- **S-T analysis (strengths-threats)** – How can our strengths be used to counteract threats that tend to hinder achievement of objectives and pursuit of opportunities?

- **W-O analysis (weaknesses-opportunities)** – How can our weaknesses be overcome to take advantage of development opportunities?

- **W-T analysis (weaknesses-threats)** – How can our weaknesses be overcome to counteract threats that tend to hinder achievement of objectives and pursuit of opportunities?

SWOT assists experienced managers in developing their critical thinking skills to make wise, well thought-out business decisions

With globalization comes a higher level of thinking and strategizing. Business will evolve in new ways. We will be teaching people "how to think" rather than "what to think." We will be fostering wealth at the level of the individual – using it to "give a man a fishing pole" rather than the fish.

> *"You want to be where the puck is going, not where it is."*
>
> ~Wayne Gretzky, ice hockey player and coach

By focusing on strategic thinking, you will enlarge your field of vision to achieve breakthrough strategic ideas.

Summary

We all conduct business in a global environment. As a result, the skills of valuing diversity and cultural sensitivity are critical to develop in you and your team members. With advances in technology and expanding marketplaces, most likely someday everyone will have virtual team members to manage. Experienced managers will have developed the ability to look past their boundaries to see how the external environment impacts the way they manage, as well as how it impacts their department, and company. They apply strategic thinking to connect what they see in the environment with their organization's strategy, customers, and colleagues.

Building Your Map
Follow-up Activities

1. **Describe your organization:** a) Industry, b) locations of offices/plants, c) products and services, d) type of customer served, e) your marketplace [local, state, country, global], f) several of your competitors

2. **Explore what your company offers for communicating long distance with virtual team members.** Establish a system for regularly communicating with and involving virtual team members.

3. **Describe why cultural diversity and cultural sensitivity are important for your department and organization.**

   _____

   _____

   _____

4. **Conduct an environmental scan for your organization. Share the details with your manager and obtain his/her insights.** Consider the factors in PESTEL: political, economic, social, technological, environmental, legal.

5. **Perform a SWOT analysis for your organization based on information you gained from PESTEL.**

Where to Go From Here
Helpful Training Topics

- ❑ Strategic planning
- ❑ Strategic thinking
- ❑ Cultural sensitivity
- ❑ SWOT analysis

THREE

AN AERIAL VIEW
Examining Your Corporate Culture

Chapter Learning Points
- Identify your organization's corporate culture
- Become a caretaker of culture

> *"I don't know anything about American history or presidents. I don't know what tailgating is! I've never been to an Olive Garden!"*
>
> ~ Emma Thompson, English actress, on the culture shock she experienced going to an American university

Culture Shock

Let's say you are planning a trip around the world to include stops in England, Russia, South Africa, and China. As you prepare for your trip, you begin to learn about the culture and customs in each country, look up the long-range weather forecast, and plan activities so you know what to pack. You know the language, food, art, music, and geography will be unique to each culture. You intellectually accept that things will be different and look forward to experiencing the differences each culture will offer.

When you get to these other countries, however, reality sets in and suddenly you miss things about your own culture that you usually take for granted—things like ice in beverages, TV shows, peanut butter, drive-thru fast food restaurants, free bathrooms, Starbucks, automatic transmission cars, stores open 24 hours, and pay-at-the-pump gas stations. You suddenly become homesick for the familiarity of your own culture, the things you took for granted. You may ask questions in an incredulous voice tone: "What do you mean there isn't a place to buy an aspirin in the middle of the night?"

What you are experiencing is culture shock. Culture shock is the feeling of disorientation experienced by someone who is suddenly subjected to an unfamiliar culture or way of life.

Can you experience culture shock in the work environment? Definitely! Even if you hire people with experience in your specific industry, they might come from an entirely different corporate culture. Your newly hired employee may assume that every organization's culture is exactly the same, and, assuming the same thing, you might not have included an explanation of your culture during the interview.

You may have heard the saying "can't see the forest for the trees." It means that if you look at things one at a time, you might not realize how each separate "tree" goes together to make a "forest." When we are too close to a situation we need to step back and get a little perspective. That is what we'll do in the rest of this chapter: step back and get a little perspective on how to define culture, how to identify the characteristics of your company's culture, and what are your managerial responsibilities as the caretakers of culture.

What Is Corporate Culture?

For most organizations, culture is an informal, shared way of perceiving life within an organization. Authors Julia Balogun and Veronica Hope Hailey define culture as "It's the way we do things around here." Many organizations specifically define their values, mission, and vision to provide a stated sense of common direction for all employees and guidelines for their day-to-day behavior.

Values define the character of a company; they describe what the company stands for. Examples of organizational values include innovation, integrity, and accountability. A mission statement defines the purpose of the organization and can include a description of its products and services and its target market. A vision statement differs from a mission in that it is future oriented and it focuses on what the organization strives to become.

Compare a few of these mission statements to see how each differs based on the organization's type of business and operating philosophies:

Google – search engine and online advertising industry. "Google's mission is to organize the world's information and make it universally accessible and useful."

MasterCard – a financial services firm. "Every day, everywhere, we use our technology and expertise to make payments safe, simple, and smart."

Here are a few reflection questions about mission statements. What is your company's mission statement? How does it compare to the mission statements listed above? What is the mission statement of your main competition and how does it differ from yours? An interesting activity is to conduct an internet search of various mission statements.

Picture a tree, some of it is visible—the leaves and branches. But much of the tree—its roots—are below ground and not readily visible. The same can be said about culture. We can read a company's values and vision and mission statements. You can observe how people interact, the layout and color of their furniture and surroundings, how people dress, the sound volume, and more. What you can't see are the "unspoken rules" that exist, which are automatic and unconscious and new employees are automatically encouraged to follow. Not until you are immersed in the culture will you learn about its "roots," and then you will probably not really be able to see them since they will be so ingrained in the way you operate.

"Culture is a little like dropping an Alka-Seltzer into a glass—you don't see it, but somehow it does something."

~ Hans Magnus Enzenberger, German author

A few more facts about culture:

- The longer the organization is in existence, the more highly developed its culture will be.
- Strong cultures reduce uncertainty for members; people know what is expected.
- The more developed the culture, the more difficult it will be to change.
- Companies with strong shared values 1) have a clear and explicit philosophy on how to conduct business and 2) have values that are known, understood, and shared by all employees.

To assist in identifying the culture of an organization, it helps to examine a variety of characteristics. Some of these characteristics are dependent on the regulatory requirements for your industry. As you read the following characteristics, think about how you can use the terminology to describe your organization:

1. **Decision making** – How much autonomy do employees have for making decisions and what are the levels of approval required? How fast does the organization make decisions? How agile is the company when faced with new ideas?

2. **Formality** – Is a clear "chain of command" established and followed? Is there an open door policy where any employee can speak with anyone in the company or must the chain of command be followed? Has the company created standard operating procedures and processes for every function? How bureaucratic are the policies and procedures?

3. **Teamwork** – Are employees encouraged to collaborate and assist one another in achieving goals? Do employees value autonomy and independent work? Does the organization have a belief that "none of us is as good as all of us?" Is collaboration or competition among individuals rewarded?

4. **Innovation** – What is the organization's tolerance for risk and change? Are policies and procedures flexible to encourage processes to be examined and streamlined? Are new ideas rushed to market or analyzed for lengthy periods of time before implementation?

5. **Conflict tolerance** – Are employees encouraged to air differences and criticism openly? Is conflict seen as a positive to avoid making the wrong decisions? Is conflict encouraged to test assumptions and avoid "group think"?

Now that you know a little more about how to describe culture, think about how you would describe your organization's culture to an applicant or new employee. Think about examples and stories that would demonstrate your culture characteristics and the "way we do things around here."

How Managers Impact Culture

In the "Guiding the Journey" chapter from *TMM*, we learned that managers are the key ingredient in creating the type of work climate where people feel energized and enjoy their work. You and your fellow managers need to be the role models for the desired culture and work climate. Managers must pay attention to culture and regularly communicate values to employees.

> *"The only thing of real importance that leaders do is to create and manage culture. If you do not manage culture, it manages you, and you may not even be aware of the extent to which this is happening."*
>
> ~Edgar Schein, professor MIT School of Business

Shaping culture is one of the most important things that managers can do, and all managerial functions directly impact the culture. Here are a few examples:

- **Staffing** – Managers with a clear understanding of their corporate culture not only hire new employees with the appropriate technical skills, they identify candidates who relate to the mission and can thrive in the culture.

- **Orientation** – Although a human resource professional typically conducts orientation, it is important that a manager connects with the new employee immediately to discuss the importance of the values and culture within the department.

- **Rewards/Recognition/Coaching/Discipline** – An organization's mission, values, and vision are merely words until reinforced by action. Culture becomes more deeply ingrained when employees see there are positive consequences (rewards/recognition) or negative consequences (discipline). These managerial reinforcement tools demonstrate that the organization is serious about its culture.

- **Communication** – Managers can impact culture by what they communicate, when they communicate, and how they communicate. Thoughts on how you are reinforcing the culture should be on your mind when sending emails, communicating one-on-one, and holding meetings.

Matching practices and procedures with the company's stated culture is important for congruency. For example, if the company's recruitment process is formal and long, you can't claim that the culture is casual and spontaneous. When the company describes its culture it will attract a specific type of candidate. It is important to ask whether these characteristics reflect the skill set of candidates the organization wants to attract. For example, if the culture is described as a team environment, it will attract team players. If new employees discover a culture lacking in cohesion and opportunities to collaborate, they will become frustrated and leave.

The website yourdictionary.com defines congruence as "the state or quality of being in agreement; correspondence; harmony." Quite often companies develop a list of value statements, and they frame them and put them on the wall, but they are not actually practiced in the workplace. Another situation that causes problems of congruency occurs when another company's best practices are implemented without considering whether they will complement your culture. What sounds like a great idea in a magazine article or professional conference turns out to be a disaster when the concept is incongruent with what makes your culture work. I've heard this described as an "organ rejection" because of the mismatch.

Examine the following situations and see if you can determine the congruency issues and consequences:

1. Your values statement includes creativity and innovation in a culture with low tolerance for risk. It takes three review committees and six levels of signatures to approve a new product. What is the result?

2. You are introducing a productivity-based bonus plan in a culture that values quality over quantity. What do you think the reaction will be?

3. Your organization has a formal, hierarchal culture. You want to implement an employee involvement strategy that encourages self-directed work teams to make decisions and question the status quo. What will be the barriers to success?

4. You have a culture that is team oriented and parental. You have always paid all benefits in full for employees and have given profit sharing to everyone. Due to cost increases, you would like to have more of a cost sharing of benefits with employees. You also want to make the profit sharing based on individual performance. What will be the reaction?

5. Your value statements say you reward and recognize individuality, but your performance reviews are based on team results. Will your team members take your value statements seriously?

6. Your company establishes a goal for a certain amount of training hours employees are expected to attend each year. In reality, the pressure to achieve results and hectic pace of the workplace isn't conducive for taking time off for training. Will immediate supervisors discourage employees from attending training because it will take them away from their work?

Before implementing new programs or procedure changes, first examine how they will impact the culture. As a change agent and keeper of your organization's culture, always ask if the change is in congruence with your culture.

Summary

Culture shock can happen when traveling to another country or when joining a new organization. Each company has its own unique culture, and it is important to identify and be able to describe the characteristics of your company's culture. In carrying out your managerial responsibilities, you are either supporting and reinforcing the culture or creating incongruence.

Building Your Map
Follow-Up Activities

1. **Culture Shock Examples**
   ❑ Think about a time when you've traveled to another country. What surprised you about the culture? What did you miss about your own culture?
   ❑ Compare two companies you've worked for in the past. How did their cultures differ? What did you expect when you went to work for each company and how did the experiences differ?
   ❑ Has a new employee ever complained, "You do so many things differently here than in my last company." How could this culture shock have been managed?

2. **Analyze Your Corporate Culture.** Reread the definition of the different culture characteristics on pages 39-40 and evaluate your organization:
   ❑ **Decision making:** ( ) Fast ( ) Moderate ( ) Slow
   ❑ **Formality:** ( ) Formal ( ) Informal
   ❑ **Teamwork:** ( ) Collaboration ( ) Individualism
   ❑ **Innovation:** ( ) High Risk ( ) Risk Averse
   ❑ **Conflict tolerance:** ( ) Encouraged ( ) Avoided

3. **List specific actions you will take to support your organization's culture when engaged in the following managerial actions:**
   ❑ Staffing: _____
   ❑ Orientation: _____
   ❑ Rewards/Recognition: _____
   ❑ Coaching/Discipline: _____
   ❑ Communication: _____

4. Think about a time when an organization implemented a change that was incongruent with their culture. What was the impact?

_____

_____

_____

Where to Go From Here
Helpful Training Topics

❑   Implementing change

❑   Understanding culture and change

❑   Communication skills

FOUR

ALL ABOARD!
Acquiring Talent

Chapter Learning Points
- Recognize characteristics of top talent
- Create onboarding for new team members

> *"There is something that is much more scarce,*
> *something finer far, something rarer than ability.*
> *It is the ability to recognize ability."*
>
> ~Elbert Hubbard, American writer and publisher

Recognizing Ability

You might not have realized it, but you have been preparing for your managerial role of selecting top talent your whole life.

Remember when you were in grade school and it was time to pick "teams" for a game? If you were the team leader you sized up your classmates and remembered their past abilities and accomplishments. Of course no one ever wanted to be the last one picked! If you were competitive and wanted your team to win, you chose the best kids for your team. If you just wanted to have fun, you picked your best friends and didn't care if your team won or lost.

Moving on to high school and college, you were probably involved in a club or sport. Now the coaches were the people who selected the best athlete for the softball team or the most talented performer for the school play or orchestra. The lesson you learned from experience or observation was when you selected the best people for the role, you would win the game or deliver an exceptional performance.

In his book *Good to Great*, Jim Collins says, "...to build a successful organization and team you must get the right people on the bus." In this metaphor, the bus is your organization; it only has so many seats just like you have only so many employees you can hire for your team. The right people are the employees with the best skills and abilities that fit the culture of your "bus." You want to make sure you not only get the right people on the bus in the first place, but you also want to keep the right people happy so they want to stay on the bus.

Quite often managers are overwhelmed by having multiple openings and feel pressured to fill positions quickly just to get the help they need. This situation may result in the "just get me a warm body" mentality, because managers feel that having anyone is better than no one on the job. However, just hiring "bodies" creates major consequences, including:

- Longer training time for new team members who don't possess the knowledge and skills necessary to do the job.

- Frustration by current team members who are first excited about a new person joining the team but then realize that he/she isn't qualified to do the job.

- Being in a constant interviewing mode because hiring unqualified people usually leads to higher turnover.

- Lack of commitment to the organization if people are quickly acquired regardless of their skill and then viewed as disposable if they don't perform. How committed would you be if you knew you were hired as a warm body because "anyone can do this job?"

> *"I am convinced that nothing we do is more important than hiring and developing people. At the end of the day you bet on people, not strategies."*
>
> ~Larry Bossidy, retired CEO and author

Talent Acquisition Process

Each organization has a unique way to manage the talent acquisition process. Your human resource department can supply you with your company's process and procedures for interviewing and selecting new team members. They may require a requisition form to begin the process.

Described below are steps I recommend to my clients. As you go through each step, remember to communicate with human resources to learn how your process differs from my recommendations to ensure you comply with your company's requirements.

Step I: Forecast staffing needs. Conduct this step before an opening becomes available to have a well thought out plan in place.

Step II: Identify critical success factors. These factors are the knowledge, skills, abilities, and culture fit that are necessary for top performance in each job.

Step III: Develop interview questions. In this step you have the opportunity to ask interviewing questions tied to the critical success factors you identified for the position.

Step IV: Interview candidates. Interviewing provides an opportunity to ask your prepared questions to determine the candidate's fit for the open position.

Step V: Realistic job preview. Reveals both the positive and negative aspects of the job and company so candidates can make an informed decision about a position.

Forecast Staffing Needs

You come to work on Monday morning and the first thing that happens is that Carl, your best employee, turns in his two-week resignation letter. Your first reaction may be "Oh no, there will be an empty seat; quick let's find another Carl to replace him." However, this thinking may not produce the best business strategy.

Before starting your recruiting effort, it is important to consider two questions: 1) Do I need to replace Carl?

and 2) Do I need someone with Carl's specific background and skills? Whether you do your own recruiting or partner with someone from the human resources department, the following factors should be considered before taking action:

- Is your department about to enter a busy or slow period? You may want to delay locating a replacement if you know the workload will soon be decreasing.

- Is the company planning to add or lose customers that would increase or decrease your workload? If you are expecting a new, large customer you may want to take this opportunity to add more than one employee from the pool of applicants.

- What is the current workload of your other staff members? If their workload is small, consider having your current staff absorb additional work or duties through reorganization instead of replacing Carl.

- What critical skills are missing from your department that a new employee could add to the department? For example, your department may need someone with specific computer software experience. Carl may have been terrific at his job, but he may have lacked a critical skill that was recently added to his job description. Taking a closer look at the skills needed for the job may lead you to look for candidates with a slightly different background.

Every organization, regardless of size, can forecast staffing needs to plan ahead to hire the right people for future openings. If you make time for planning, you will reduce hiring time and cost, lower training costs for new employees, and have a more stable and motivated workforce.

Forecasting staffing needs is an ongoing process that is conducted before you become desperate to "fill a seat." Begin with an analysis of past turnover, determining how many employees typically leave each year either voluntarily or involuntarily. The next step is to estimate how the workload will change for the upcoming year based on number of clients or changes in equipment or processes that will increase efficiency. The last step is to analyze the skills needed currently and in the future based on either the job description or, if your organization doesn't use descriptions, a list of duties and skills needed to perform the job. Consider this simple example:

Current workforce	15
Typical annual turnover	3
New positions to be added this year	2

Your forecast reveals that you will probably need to hire 5 people this year. Further analysis of the job function reveals that employees will have more frequent customer interaction. You decide to add customer service experience to your recruitment criteria and also make training plans for your current staff.

> *"People are not your most important asset. The right people are."*
>
> ~Jim Collins, business consultant and author

Identify Critical Success Factors

You are ready to go out and find the right people, and identifying critical success factors will assist you in accomplishing this step. Critical success factors include those skills, abilities, and previous experience that will turn a candidate into a successful, productive team member. Success factors can also relate to education, training, technical ability, as well as interpersonal skills, culture fit, values match, and the ability to work required hours.

As previously mentioned, a good place to begin looking for critical success factors is the job description. Many acceptable formats for job descriptions exist, so you should always check with your organization for their specific format requirements. Here is a sample job description for a receptionist. See if you can identify the critical success factors:

Job title: Receptionist

Summary: Responsible for greeting visitors to XYZ Company in person and over the phone in a manner that provides a positive impression of the organization.

Essential Duties and Responsibilities:
1. Greet visitors, making them feel welcome and following check-in guidelines.
2. Contact employee representatives to indicate that they have a visitor.
3. Answer incoming calls and determine the proper person required before transferring the call.
4. Take messages as required.

5. Accept delivery of office packages and mail.
6. Sort incoming mail by department.

Required Knowledge, Skills, and Abilities:
1. Interpersonal skills to make visitors and callers feel welcome
2. Professional verbal communication skills with the ability to use proper grammar
3. Ability to handle multiple priorities
4. Ability to hear over the phone and sit for long periods of time

Education and Experience:
- High school diploma or equivalent
- Prior experience using multi-line telephone system preferred
- Prior industry experience preferred to understand caller requests for information

Based on this job description, you probably identified the following critical success factors for our receptionist position:

❑ Interpersonal skills
❑ Communication skills
❑ Previous experience interacting with the public
❑ Ability to handle multiple priorities (telephone ringing, taking messages, clients entering the lobby, deliveries being made, etc.)
❑ High school degree or equivalent
❑ Previous experience in the industry to understand jargon of callers and visitors

Where else can you find critical success factors? Your culture analysis! For example, if your culture is considered very formal with a strict business dress code and employees must adhere to standard operating procedures, it would be important that the receptionist you hire will thrive in this environment. A relaxed person who spontaneously makes decisions and likes to wear T-shirts and flip-flops might not be a good fit.

You will be able to determine if a candidate has some of your critical success factors by simply reviewing a resume or job application. Other factors must be determined during the interview.

Develop Interview Questions

My preferred type of interview questions is behavioral-based, which are questions based on the philosophy that "past behavior is one of the best predictors of future behavior." So instead of answering "what if" questions, the candidate has to respond based on what they actually did in the past. If a candidate's actions made them successful in the past, chances are they will behave the same in the future and create success for your organization.

Continuing our receptionist example, a few behavior-based questions to consider asking for the critical success factors we identified include:

1. Describe a particular face-to-face customer interaction experience where you were able to solve his or her problem to their satisfaction.
2. Tell me about a situation where you had to handle multiple priorities in a fast-paced environment.

Some of your candidates may not be accustomed to these types of interview questions and may answer in generalities. For example, you may receive this answer to the first question: "I'm always helpful to customers and enjoy solving their problems." At this point you smile and redirect the candidate by saying, "That is great. Can you give me a recent example of what you specifically did to solve that customer's problem?" Follow-up questions might be necessary to ensure you receive a specific example.

Let's Pause for a Legal Review

In the "License to Manage" chapter of **TMM**, we learned five basic rights of employees and were directed to important federal agency websites that all managers need to view. One of those websites is for the Equal Employment Opportunity Commission (EEOC.gov). If you haven't already visited the site, you should have this on your "to-do" list. Here are a few excerpts from the EEOC.gov site related to our "All Aboard!" chapter.

> *Under the laws enforced by EEOC, it is illegal to discriminate against an applicant because of that person's race, color, religion, sex (including pregnancy), national origin, age (40 or older), disability, or genetic information. This includes the wording in job advertisements, use of recruitment sources, your application process, and your hiring decisions process.*
>
> *If an employer requires job applicants to take a test, the test must be necessary and related to the job and the employer may not exclude people of a*

particular race, color, religion, sex (including pregnancy), national origin, or individuals with disabilities. In addition, the employer may not use a test that excludes applicants age 40 or older if the test is not based on a reasonable factor other than age.

If a job applicant with a disability needs an accommodation (such as a sign language interpreter) to apply for a job, the employer is required to provide the accommodation, so long as the accommodation does not cause the employer significant difficulty or expense.

Knowledge and compliance with these regulations protects your company from complaints to federal agencies and possibly lawsuits.

Interview Candidates

Employment interviews are conducted for three reasons:

1. To evaluate a candidate's suitability for a specific opening in the organization
2. To provide information about the position to a candidate
3. To create a good image for the organization, by making a positive, lasting impression for the candidate

Depending on your company's process, you may first conduct a telephone screening interview with a few key questions from your interview question list. A telephone screen is a good method for assessing communication skills. Telephone screening saves both you and the candidate time because it quickly assesses a basic skills match. After asking a few key questions, you can then schedule an in-person interview or thank the applicant and end the call.

Both your non-verbal and verbal skills are important when conducting the interview. Your non-verbal skills, such as smiling and nodding encouragement during answers, will put the applicant at ease. You will obtain the maximum amount of information for your hiring decision if your applicants feel comfortable during the interview. Your verbal skills will assist you in getting answers to your questions. Use a pleasant non-threatening tone of voice, and be careful not to give the answer away in your question.

To gain the most information from the applicant, the interview should be structured so that the applicant is speaking 80 percent of the time and the interviewer 20 percent. Your interview should be structured with a definite opening, middle, and closing. During the opening you are introducing yourself, your position, and providing the applicant with the agenda for the interview. The purpose of the opening is to make the applicant comfortable and relaxed.

The middle of your interview is the time when you ask your behavioral-based questions to determine whether the applicant has the required critical skills to be successful in the open position.

During the closing part of your interview, the applicant should be provided with the opportunity to ask questions. Then it is important to discuss what happens next. Include the following in this step:

- Discuss when you expect to make the hiring decision.
- Discuss other process steps, including such items as realistic job preview, second interview, drug test, and reference check.
- Thank the applicant.

> _"When I meet successful people I ask 100 questions as to what they attribute their success to. It is usually the same: persistence, hard work and hiring good people."_
>
> ~Kiana Tom, fitness television host

Realistic Job Preview

While you are trying to determine if candidates possess the critical skills for your open position, they are trying to decide whether they will be happy and fulfilled if they decide to join your company.

Companies that supply a realistic job preview (RJP) for candidates tend to eliminate disappointment for new employees. Candidates will have expectations about a job based on their previous company experiences or what they believe they hear during the interview process, and will make assumptions that may not be correct. These expectations may be about the work environment as well as the job content. Including a RJP in your hiring process helps alleviate any feelings of dissatisfaction and regret employees may have if the job is different from their expectations.

A RJP not only tells candidates what it's like to work in the open job, it lets them experience it. For example, when I was VP Human Resources at a manufacturing company, we hired people to work on an assembly line. We noticed a pattern that many new employees would not return to their work station after their first break. The joke became that we had an escape tunnel in the restroom since the new employees were never seen again after break! We decided to implement a RJP for candidates where they watched the assembly line after the interview and even let them try the process for a few minutes. This example demonstrates a show-tell-try approach to RJP. Candidates not only had the opportunity to hear about the job, they had a chance to see it and do it. Then, if they were offered the position, they were in a much better position to accept or decline, which lowered our turnover rate in the department.

What type of realistic job preview can you create for your candidates? At a minimum, it is important to show the candidates the work environment during a tour of the facility. During the tour, the interviewer can point out aspects of the work area, the pace of the work, and even the noise level. Some organizations create videos depicting the work environment and other unique characteristics of the job. Another option is to let candidates meet with current incumbents in the job to ask questions.

Incorporating a RJP in your hiring process allows candidates to feel in control of their job search, and the result is an increase in job satisfaction and organizational commitment among new hires.

Ultimately, an effective RJP results in lower turnover and hiring costs.

Hiring Virtual Team Members

Let's apply the concepts we discussed to hiring virtual or long distance team members:

Step I: Forecast staffing needs. Is the team member you are replacing currently a virtual employee? Is this the most effective staffing option?

Step II: Identify critical success factors. In addition to the skills and abilities required by the position, you will need to probe for the skills required for working virtually, such as self-motivation, the ability to keep focused, and communicating long distance.

Step III: Develop interview questions. The questions you ask should include the virtual critical success factors listed above. An example question would be, "Tell me about a time when you had to work independently to accomplish your goals."

Step IV: Interview candidates. The initial interview can be over the phone, but you may wish to also include a video conference call.

Step V: Provide realistic job preview. Think creatively to describe not only the job but what it is like to work virtually. Some organizations produce short videos of current virtual employees, describing how they communicate and organize their work as well as the benefits and challenges of working long distance.

Onboarding New Hires

What do you do when a valued member of your team decides to leave your company? Do you throw a party, give them a card everyone has signed, and have a cake? Team members go through this effort because they want to show the person leaving that they valued them and will miss them.

Now think about what you do for a new team member. This new person is in a position to make a significant contribution to your organization for what will hopefully be a long time and therefore should also be immediately shown they are valued. Why not use the same party ideas you use for exiting members with new people?

Let's follow a tale of two employees—Julie and Carol—who are each starting a new job today.

Tale I: Julie arrives about 10 minutes early for work in a new outfit. She waits by the receptionist for her new manager to come and get her as employees rush by her on the way to their workstations and meetings. About 20 minutes past her start time, her new manager walks by, stops abruptly, and says, "Oh, you're Julie, right? Is today the day you are starting? I completely forgot about it. Follow me and I'll show you to your desk." When they arrive at her desk it looks like it was raided by pirates, stripped of basic office supplies and with dust gathered in corners where bins used to be located. The manager calls to the person in the next cubicle and says, "Maria, this is Julie, our new team member. She will sit with you and watch you work today." Maria rolls her eyes and says, "Fine, but I don't have time to show her anything today since I'm on a tight deadline."

Tale 2: Carol arrives about 10 minutes early for her new job, also in a new outfit. She waits by the receptionist for her new manager to come and get her, and as employees enter the building for the day, several stop by and introduce themselves saying things like, "welcome aboard" and "you must be Carol." Her manager arrives on time to greet her and bring her to her desk, which has a plaque with her name. Her desk is clean and fully stocked with office supplies. Directions on how to use the phone and sign onto her computer are displayed along with a sign that says "Welcome Carol!" that every team member has signed. Susan, one of her team members, is waiting for her. The manager introduces them and says, "Susan is your first-day guide today, and here is your agenda. Notice that we set up a time for you to meet with everyone to get to know them, and Susan will be taking you to lunch today." During the afternoon break, the whole team shares a cake that welcomes Carol to the department.

What are Julie and Carol each going to tell their friends and family about their first day when they get home? Remember each person has just completed a job search and another company may have been a little slow in making a job offer. What will each of them say if they are offered another job with a week or two of starting with your organization? Do you think their treatment on their first day, week, or month will make a difference in their answer?

During the first few weeks on a new job, people are trying to answer the questions "Did I make the right decision in accepting this job?" and "Is this the type of company where I will feel accepted and given the opportunity to be successful?" Managers should immediately form a connection with the new employees so the answers to those two questions are "YES!" Virtual employees also have these two concerns plus they are worried that they will feel "lost in space" because they are not located in the same physical place as their manager.

In the 1930s, a researcher named Konrad Lorenz became very interested in imprinting, and he managed to prove that geese and ducks really will become attached to the first moving thing they see, whether or not it is another duck. He managed to raise a flock of geese that imprinted on him and followed him everywhere.

We can apply Lorenz's imprinting experiment to new employee onboarding. To build that strong connection, managers need to connect with their new employees on their first day. Starting out with a welcoming, trusting relationship will establish a lasting attachment to the manager, team members, and the organization. Here are a few ideas:

- **Checklists** – Design an onboarding checklist to make sure that important information is covered and the experience is designed to immediately connect with the new employee. A good source in developing your checklist are recently hired employees who can advise you what they liked about their first weeks on the job and what specifically was most helpful in getting acclimated.

- **Introductions** – Create opportunities for new employees to get to know their team members and frequent contacts in the company. Since everyone is busy, this may not happen naturally, so it is important to schedule interaction time on your on-boarding schedule. Let your current employees know when a new employee is starting and encourage your team members to welcome the new member at every opportunity. If virtual employees cannot travel to the home office, schedule video conferencing calls with their most frequent contacts so they can start to place a "face with a name."

- **Imprinting** – Although your company's human resource department may conduct the orientation, you can establish yourself as the "go to" person" for questions by following up with your new employee in order to connect what they learned with department specifics. Schedule time to review the onboarding checklist with your new employee to see how the process is working and how he or she is feeling about the new job. The scheduled frequency you have for phone or video conferences with virtual employees should be increased during their first few months on the job. Remember what we learned about Lorenz's geese experiment!

In Chapter 6, "Commitment to the Journey... Building Engagement at Work," we will explore the importance of having an engaged workforce. Engagement begins on the new employee's first day of work. People are excited about their new job and arrive engaged. Keeping employees engaged is another challenge for another chapter.

Summary

Hiring the right people for your department is one of your most important managerial tasks. Experienced managers understand the critical success factors for their department and apply the process required by their organization. They also understand the importance of supplying a realistic job preview during the hiring process so that candidates can make an informed decision on whether the opening is the best fit for them. Finally, experienced managers create onboarding plans to immediately engage the new employee and to minimize those first-day jitters that can come with starting a new job.

Building Your Map
Follow-up Activities

1. **Forecast your staffing needs for next year**
   a) Average headcount for your department

   b) Average turnover for your department

   c) Estimate of headcount growth or decrease based on new clients or technology or other projected changes

2. **Locate a job description for a position you may have to recruit for in the near future.** Circle all the items that can be considered critical success factors for candidates. Make a list of these factors

   ❑ _____

   ❑ _____

   ❑ _____

3. **Write behavioral-based interview questions.** Make a chart with critical success factors on the left and your interview question on the right. Review your questions with a member of human resources to ensure legal compliance.

4. **Create a realistic job preview for candidates who interview for this position.** Remember the show-tell-do approach.

5. **Lead a brainstorming session with your team members on how to create a welcoming atmosphere for new employees.**

6. **Create an onboarding checklist.** Include connection time with coworkers and frequent contacts, training schedule, and follow up time with you.

Where to Go From Here
Helpful Training Topics

- ☐ Interview skills
- ☐ Listening skills
- ☐ Communication skills
- ☐ Facilitation skills

FIVE

ALL HANDS ON DECK...
Building a Strong Team

Chapter Learning Points
- Understand characteristics of effective teams
- Build a team environment

> *"You can't play a symphony alone; it takes an orchestra to play it."*
>
> ~Navjot Singh Sidhu, former Indian cricketer turned politician

Team Synergy

Team members enter their work area, and their navigational map is neatly placed at each work station. By reading their map, they know their current location and the end result of their journey together. Their map also shows where the rest of their team members are located. But this isn't a normal map with such things room numbers and names, or longitude and latitude. It is a musical score showing the music of all instruments and voices in a composition, and the team is an orchestra. The musicians have their own piece of music, and they are surrounded by their peers who are playing the same or different instruments.

69

Musicians can play a whole beautiful piece of music alone, but when they come together, synergy is created where "the whole is greater than the sum of its parts." A symphony is richer than solo performances, with the various instruments blending together to create a harmonious combination of sounds that can't be duplicated with just one instrument.

The orchestra conductor is similar to a manager of a team. Most orchestra conductors begin their careers specializing in an instrument. To effectively lead the orchestra, they need to change their view of their role from specialist to conductor, ensuring all instruments are played perfectly at the right time to produce amazing music. Can you imagine the orchestra leader moving one of the violin players out of a chair and taking over in the middle of the symphony? Managers also begin their careers as specialists and are typically promoted from within their department. They also have to change their view of their role from doer to manager, ensuring all team members are performing to the best of their abilities.

If a conductor doesn't set the team's direction, understand the strengths of each team member, and know how the team is set up, the probabilities are slim that the team will make beautiful music. The conductor needs to keep an eye on both the musical score and the musicians, giving direction by gestures for the pace of the music and when it's time for various musicians to join in and start playing. Luckily, managers have the ability to communicate verbally in their role instead of using only a baton to provide direction to their team.

Definition and Importance of Teamwork

More and more, organizations require the ability to work in teams. Whether a group of people are assembled for a specific project or work together on a regular basis, the ability to work effectively with people who may have different approaches is essential.

Teamwork is the process of working collaboratively with a group of people to achieve a goal. Imagine that a team of your employees get together and, by using each person's strengths, develop a breakthrough idea that catapults your organization to the next level. Yes, amazing results can happen.

> *"Never doubt that a small group of thoughtful, committed people can change the world. Indeed, it is the only thing that ever has."*
>
> ~Margaret Mead, American cultural anthropologist

The challenge managers' face is twofold: 1) Create teamwork among the group they manage, and 2) Draw the connection of how their work contributes to both internal and external customers so the value of teamwork throughout the organization is realized.

A team is a group of people who come together to achieve a common goal. The benefits of teamwork are easy to recognize when you can link the part you play in achieving your company's bottom-line goals.

A manager's job is to help team members find their own strengths and the diverse strengths of the others on the team. Have you ever played Trivial Pursuit? The object of the game is to move around the board by correctly answering trivia questions. Questions are split into six categories, with each one having its own identifying color. In the classic version of *Trivial Pursuit*, the *Genus* edition, these are geography, (blue), entertainment (pink), history (yellow), arts & literature (brown), science & nature (green), and sports & leisure (orange). Think about a time when you've played as an individual. There were probably categories that you knew the answers to right away; others you might not have had a clue as to what they were talking about. It would take me forever to get a blue piece, as geography is not one of my strengths. But, if you play in a team comprised of different knowledge strengths, you increase your chances of winning by utilizing the expertise of others.

A great team works that way too. When you value the skills and knowledge of others, and listen to them because they do have a different point of view, you end up with better results.

> *"Teamwork is the ability to work together towards a common vision. The ability to direct individual accomplishments towards organizational objectives. It is the fuel that allows common people to attain uncommon results."*
>
> ~Andrew Carnegie, American industrialist

Teamwork and Innovation

Teamwork is a major contributor to innovation when you can harness the unique strengths and approaches of each team member. Much like members of a relay team, each team should feel free to take on the role that best meets its talents.

Wiley Publishing's **Team Dimensions** program identifies five team talents. Listed below are ways to capitalize on team talents when addressing typical team challenges:

- **Creating New Ideas** – Does your team create new "out-of-the-box" ideas or just recycle old ideas? Encourage the creators on your team to contribute new ideas in an imaginative and abstract way.

- **Advancing New Ideas** – Do your team's good ideas "die on the vine?" Perhaps your team needs to encourage team members who are skilled at interacting with others to spread the word and get people energized about new solutions.

- **Refining New Ideas** – Does your team rush to implement new ideas without fine-tuning? Your team may need to encourage participation from those individuals who focus on analyzing and testing ideas for merit and possible errors.

- **Executing New Ideas** – Do your team members have great ideas that never get implemented? Your team may need to recognize those individuals who focus on creating and implementing realistic, detailed-oriented plans.

Identifying team members who see a value in all the innovation talents of creating, advancing, refining, and executing will focus your team on doing the right thing at the right time for breakthrough innovation.

Does this story sound familiar?

After months of research and planning, you have developed a breakthrough idea that will dramatically improve your organization. You have a vision of what it will look like and how to get there. You announce the vision to your team with great fanfare, and everyone appears to be on board. However, after a few weeks, nothing seems to be changing and the idea fizzles. What happened?

> *"No matter how clearly you may see the picture of your improved future, without aligning others, your vision will remain a pipe dream."*
>
> ~*The Work of Leaders*, Wiley Publishing 2013

Statistics show that about 70 percent of change initiatives are not successful. Quite often new concepts fail because the team, who must execute the new strategy, is not aligned around the change. While the definition of the word align is to "bring into cooperation and agreement," the key is agreement. Change can be painful and confusing, and takes a lot of energy. If your team doesn't agree with the new vision, why should it exert the effort needed to execute it?

Here are a few tips to move your vision into reality by creating team alignment:

- **Communicate** – Before making a big vision announcement, create talking points with what people need to know and also what they will want to know. Encourage questions and suggestions.

- **Express Excitement for the Future** – What is your voice tone and body language portraying about the idea? Are you excited, bored, distracted? UCLA Professor Emeritus Albert Mehrabian's famous research reveals that people communicate more with their body language (55%) and voice tone (38%) than with their words (7%). If you manage employees remotely, you lose the body language part of your message.

- **Establish Role Clarity** – Team members will need to know what they are supposed to do and *why*. Role clarity conversations about how new initiatives will impact the members personally and how their responsibilities will contribute to the implementation are critical.

- **Patience** – While you may have been living and breathing the development of your new vision for several months, your team members have just learned about it. Patience is important to allow people to play "catch up" with everything you know.

Effective leaders not only develop breakthrough visions, they develop aligned teams committed to executing the vision.

Ineffective Teamwork

Teamwork is ineffective when 1) team members are not open and honest, 2) there is disagreement with a decision or the direction of the group, and 3) people don't see themselves as part of a team at all.

> *"Trust is knowing that when a team member does push you, they're doing it because they care about the team."*
>
> ~Patrick Lencioni, *The Five Dysfunctions of a Team: A Leadership Fable*

The term **Abilene paradox** was first introduced by management expert Jerry B. Harvey. In an Abilene paradox, a group of people collectively decide on a course of action that is counter to the preferences of many of the individuals in the group. The situation involves a common breakdown of group communication in which members mistakenly believe their own opinions are different from what the group wants, and therefore do not raise objections and go along with the first suggestion a team member makes. A common phrase relating to the Abilene paradox is having a desire to not "rock the boat." When team members have personal qualms about the decision, they need courage and must trust their team members to be able to speak up and voice concerns.

Unfortunately some employees don't see themselves as part of a team; they see only the results of their own work as the goal. This lack of teamwork can be seen in teams of front-line employees as well as executive teams.

Let's see a snapshot of a leadership team in action and see if you can pick out examples of teamwork or the lack of teamwork.

Tim, the CEO of a small but growing manufacturing company, is frustrated. He recently recruited Sandy, a high-achieving vice president of sales with industry experience and extensive contacts. After just two months at the company, Sandy landed a large customer whose orders will double their monthly sales production. Unfortunately, their new customer's first order didn't ship on time and was short the quantity ordered. The customer called Tim this morning, very upset and threatened to pull business if things didn't improve. Tim calls a staff meeting to get to the bottom of the problem.

After Tim starts the meeting with the bad news from their new client, he sees a variety of expressions from his team members seated around the conference table. Sandy is angry and speaks first: "I can't believe all my hard work and relationship with this client is in jeopardy. Maybe I made a mistake in coming to this company. I would like to know what went wrong with this simple order!"

Sally, the shipping manager simply shrugs her shoulders and says, "Hey, the product has to get to me on time if you want us to ship it on time." She then starts checking messages on her mobile phone, tuning out everyone else at the meeting.

Don, the vice president of operations, looks angry. He says, "I tried to tell you that we weren't yet equipped to handle the increased volume for this client. We're waiting for the new equipment from Germany to be delivered and installed, and the human resources department hasn't finished hiring the increased staff we need. I wasn't involved in this decision at the beginning, and then when I was brought in after the fact, you didn't listen to my objections." Don continues under his breath to say, "Typical sales mentality: over promise and then blame operations when we can't deliver."

Sandy throws her arms in the air in frustration and looks as if she is ready to walk out of the room. Wayne, the vice president of customer service, senses the tension and tries to smooth things over. "We shouldn't be fighting amongst ourselves," he says. "Let's all calm down and stop this conflict."

Tim decides this meeting isn't productive, so he ends the meeting by telling his group to send him their ideas on how to keep their new customer by Friday.

What areas of teamwork and lack of teamwork did you discover in this story? What is the impact of a dysfunctional leadership team on the rest of the workforce and organization?

Here are a few items that you probably identified from the story as lacking in teamwork:

- **When managers bash and complain about one another.** This tactic is a particularly damaging habit when we speak ill of our peers and/or boss with other employees. Bashing and complaining are also signs of managerial immaturity.

- **When managers avoid each other so as to prevent working with each other.** Employees are observant, and they pick up on the negative vibes that avoidance puts out.

- **When managers compete (expressing positions) instead of collaborating (expressing interests).** Collaborating means listening to and valuing the opinions of other team members. Competing involves the win-lose approach where team members only look for ways to win their position.

- **When managers pontificate impressive visions but fail to back these intentions up with aligned practices, measurements, and reinforcements.** A successful team aligns its individual goals with the overall team goal. The team sees the connection between what they do as individuals and the greater good of the organization.

> *"A boat doesn't go forward if each one is rowing their own way."*
>
> ~Swahili proverb

Think about the effective and ineffective teams you've been a part of in the past. People report how exciting it is to be a member of an effective team; they feel a sense of accomplishment and camaraderie that lasts long past membership in the team. You probably were excited about going to team meetings knowing they were going to be productive and intellectually stimulating. If you've ever been a part of an ineffective team, you probably wanted to avoid team meetings, knowing you would just feel frustrated and discouraged at the lack of accomplishment.

Consider your participation on various teams over the years. See if you can recognize your team members' behaviors either in Team A or Team B:

Team A has team members who:
- Tap into the skills and opinions of all team members.
- End discussions with clear and specific resolutions and calls to action.
- Make better, faster decisions.
- Achieve buy-in from everyone and focus on the right issues.
- Are personally invested, accountable, and engaged in achieving results.
- Aren't afraid to speak up when they think the team is going in the wrong direction.
- Trust the team to discuss their strengths and weaknesses and are able to ask for help when needed.

Team B has team members who:
- Are unwilling to brainstorm and compromise, share ideas, and support one another.
- Waste time on politics, personal attacks, and destructive conflict.
- Revisit discussions and decisions again and again.
- Avoid face-to-face discussions and vent in the hallway.
- Miss deadlines and key deliverables.
- Blame others when mistakes are made instead of reaching out to provide assistance.
- Act passive-aggressively by agreeing to a course of action in meetings but then taking different actions back on the job.

Did any of these characteristics sound familiar? Most people will prefer to work on Team A because we want to be part of a collaborative team that achieves success. If we're honest about it, how many of us are currently part of a Team B right now, are unhappy about their unproductive interactions and lack of results, but continue on, day after day? Many of us see the problems within the team and are not sure how to fix it, and if we do see the solution we would need the cooperation of everyone on the team to make the change. Team B doesn't appear to be too cooperative!

Tips for Improving Teamwork

Many organizations plan team-building programs only to be disappointed in the results. It's not enough to have a shared experience in a ropes course, going to an amusement park, or participating in a community improvement project day. Participants will have a good time, but positive changes are not carried over to the day-to-day interaction in the workplace. To be effective, team-building programs should contain three elements: action, reflection, and implementation.

- The Action phase, which includes the planned fun activities, should be designed to address workplace issues. Goals should be established to improve such areas as communication, problem solving, planning, and goal orientation. The Action phase should also be designed to consider the needs and interests of the participants. Adult learners want to know the purpose and why they are being asked to participate in activities.

- After the activity, a facilitator should gather the team together to lead a discussion in the Reflection phase. Participants reflect on what occurred and what they learned during the activity.

- Finally, the facilitator should focus on the connections that can be made from the Action activity to what was learned during the Reflection discussion to Implementation of lessons learned and improvements to carry back to the workplace.

Another method to improve teamwork is to create team ground rules. To create ground rules, ask every team member to contribute ideas on how the team should operate and how members should behave and interact. Established ground rules are usually posted somewhere for all team members to regularly see, especially during team meetings, to remind everyone what was decided.

Ground rules should be reached by consensus. Consensus is defined as being able to "buy into" the decision. The final decision made by the team may not have been your first choice, but if you believe your opinion was heard and respected by the rest of the team during the discussion, you willingly support the decision publicly and privately.

One of the benefits of ground rules is that they establish specific expectations. Using grounds to provide feedback to others if expectations are not met becomes easier.

Sample ground rules include:

1. Begin and end all meetings on time.
2. Withhold debate and criticism when generating ideas.
3. Make every effort to meet commitments. E-mails will be sent prior to the due date when action item commitments cannot be met.
4. Foster trust and open communication by developing relationships with fellow team members.
5. Provide constructive feedback. We will avoid being defensive and give feedback in a constructive manner.

Here are a few other team building ideas you can use during team meetings:

Effective and Ineffective Teams – At the start of your next team meeting, pose the question: "Is our team as effective as we want it to be?" Give team members the list of Team A and Team B characteristics and ask them to assess your team's current behaviors. Finally, create an action plan for improvement. Just think, work can actually be more pleasurable and less stressful!

Team Scavenger Hunt – Ask each team member to provide you with an interesting little-known fact about him or herself. Create a document with everyone's items and ask team members to place names next to each item. Encourage discussion and elaboration about each story.

Team Sharing

> *"Trust the people in the organization – the people in the best position to improve a business are the people in the job every day."*
>
> ~Jack Welch, former GE CEO

Start each meeting with a question designed to learn more about each other as people and help them find commonalities. Be sure to pick questions that wouldn't make someone uncomfortable or alienated. After you model the first few, encourage team members to submit question ideas. Question examples: In what city and state were you born? What is your favorite movie and why? Who is your favorite author? What was your college major? When you were a child, what did you want to be "when you grew up"? What are your hobbies? What was your favorite vacation? If you didn't work in your current occupation or industry, what would your occupation be?

Trust Building – Lead a team discussion of "trust builders" and "trust busters." Team members describe examples in each category, such as always meeting commitments under trust builder and taking credit for someone else's idea under trust buster. Make a list during the discussion and then ask for examples of when they have seen trust builders and trust busters in action on a team. Consider adding ideas to your team ground rules.

Role Sharing – Team members summarize their roles and goals on the team this year followed by three things that others could do to support them.

Behavior Styles – Have team members complete a behavioral assessment such as Wiley Publishing's *DiSC Workplace*. Have team members describe their teamwork strengths and hold one-on-one discussions on how they can best work with each other's style preferences.

"If you could get all the people in an organization rowing in the same direction, you could dominate any industry, in any market, against any competition at any time."

~Patrick Lencioni, author of *The Five Dysfunctions of a Team*

Team Building for Virtual Teams

Teams benefit from getting together and socializing to build team spirit and trust. But what do you do when some of your team members don't work at a central site?

You can still make an effort to include virtual employees in team building even though it's not exactly the same as being in the same room. For example, if it's "ice cream day" at work, send ice cream or a gift card to your virtual employee. Try to capture the getting-to-know-you-better spirit of teamwork by holding meetings that don't just focus on goals. Almost every one of the team-building activity suggestions can be done via video conference with the whole team.

Lastly, if you fly the virtual team member in for a business meeting, leave time for them to socialize with the people they interact with the most to build stronger relationships.

Summary

Building a strong team that values each member's strengths is a critical skill for experienced managers. Effective teams contribute to innovation and workplace satisfaction of team members. Managers need to be proactive in creating an atmosphere of teamwork and collaboration through various team development activities.

Building Your Map
Follow-up Activities

1. **Think about your experience with various teams throughout your career.** Make a list of characteristics of effective and ineffective teams.

2. **Assess your current team.** Are the characteristics of your team more like Team A or Team B? Develop a plan to improve teamwork.

_____

_____

_____

3. **Assess your current team members. List people who have strengths in each area of team talents:**
   - ☐ Creating _____
   - ☐ Advancing _____
   - ☐ Refining _____
   - ☐ Executing _____

4. **Does your team have ground rules?** Facilitate a team discussion to create ground rules.

5. **Conduct a team-building activity.** Follow the action, reflection, and implementation formula.

Where to Go From Here
Helpful Training Topics

- [ ] *Team Dimensions*, a Wiley Product
- [ ] *Five Behaviors of a Cohesive Team*, a Wiley Product
- [ ] Communication skills
- [ ] Team-building skills
- [ ] Facilitation skills

SIX

COMMITMENT TO THE JOURNEY
Building Engagement at Work

Chapter Learning Points
- Define employee engagement
- Create an environment that engages others

> *"Engaged employees stay for what they give (they like their work); disengaged employees stay for what they get (favorable job conditions, growth opportunities, job security)."*
>
> ~Blessing White's *The State of Employee Engagement*

What Is *Employee Engagement*?

Three college friends met at their local coffee shop to discuss a weekend trip. They knew that with their busy lives after college, if they didn't work at keeping in touch, they would slowly drift away from each other. They created The Three Amigos Adventure Weekend to maintain their close friendship, and they've kept it up for the last four years since graduation. Matt was the first to arrive, armed with a couple of brochures and online reviews of possible trip locations. He quickly grabbed a table where they could talk without interruption. George arrived on time, ordered coffee, and nodded pleasantly as Matt excitedly explained some of his ideas. Brad arrived 15 minutes late and continued to text as he ordered coffee and arrived at their table. When he finally greeted his two friends he began the conversation with the fact that his promotion was keeping him so busy he probably couldn't join them this year and he had to leave in 20 minutes. Brad's comments influences George to consider that maybe he is also too busy to go away this year.

Which one of these friends is fully engaged in planning their next adventure? Wikipedia defines employee engagement as "a concept that is generally viewed as managing discretionary effort. That is, when employees have choices, they will act in a way that furthers their organization's interests. An engaged employee is a person who is fully involved in and enthusiastic about his or her work."

Curt Coffman, co-author of the book *First Break All the Rules*, identifies three types of engagement:

- **Engaged Employees** – Are productive, goal oriented, and connected to the organization's mission.
- **Not Engaged Employees** – Do just enough to "get by." They show up but do not take initiative.
- **Actively Disengaged Employees** – Are unhappy in their work and with the organization to the point of disrupting the productivity of others.

In our opening story, we can see that Matt is engaged in planning the weekend, George is just going along and not engaged, and Brad is activity disengaged. We know that Matt is engaged by his preparation for the meeting and his excitement. Notice how easily George, who is someone not engaged, can become influenced to change to the actively disengaged side. However, George could also have moved over to the engaged side. Can you recognize some of your team members in this example?

Engaged employees go the extra mile, talk positively about the company, plan to stay with company, and develop ideas to improve.

Why Care about Engagement?

> *"Highly engaged employees outperform their disengaged counterparts by a whopping 20-28 percentage points."*
>
> ~The Conference Board: "Employee Engagement, A Review of Current Research and Its Implications"

Think about a time when you felt engaged at work. What did it feel like...what did you accomplish? Did you feel energized, with the ability to see through problems to develop innovative solutions? Did you feel you could accomplish miraculous results and outperform all your goals? What if all your employees were fully engaged...what would that do for your overall business results?

Research confirms a link between key business outcomes such as customer engagement, profitability, efficiency/innovation, sales growth, and employee engagement. Doesn't that make sense? It takes an engaged employee to provide the type of service that results in customer satisfaction and retention. It is tough to "fake" happiness *in* your work when you are unhappy *at* work.

There was a time when organizations were concerned with employee satisfaction, which is basically how content or happy employees are with their job. The focus of employee satisfaction initiatives was, therefore, how to make employees happy, believing "happy employees are productive employees." Organizations started noticing that quite often managers were so focused on keeping employees happy that they became reluctant to implement changes, create stretch goals, or hold employees accountable for their performance for fear it would make them "unhappy." This classic example shows what happens when you measure and focus on the wrong thing. The better focus is "happy *and* engaged employees."

Therefore the critical measurement is engagement, not just satisfaction. If your highly engaged employees can't thrive in your environment, one of two things will happen: they will become frustrated and move into the not engaged category, or they will give up totally and leave your organization where they can become successful elsewhere. Employee retention is a good first step. Retaining your engaged employees is the ultimate goal.

Barriers to Engagement

Think about your newly hired team members. When you hire new employees, they are excited and fully engaged on their first day. So, what can happen that flips the switch for that person from engaged to disengaged?

Engagement barriers are those things that prevent someone from being engaged at work. Although there may be several reasons causing the disengagement, they typically fall within three categories: unfulfilled expectations, organizational changes, and personal circumstances. Think about one of your team members who appears disengaged as you review the barriers to engagement listed below:

Unfulfilled Expectations
❏ Received less training than expected
❏ Provided with less decision-making authority than expected
❏ The job has either doesn't encourage teamwork or lacks independent work
❏ The company fails to provide promotional, advancement, or learning opportunities

Organizational Changes
❏ Job expectations have changed
❏ New rules or procedures were introduced
❏ Shortage of resources has occurred
❏ Workload has either increased or decreased
❏ Work hours have changed
❏ A new manager or team members have been hired

Personal Circumstances
❏ The team member's personal circumstances have changed, including marriage, divorce, birth of a child, child in college, spouse was promoted or laid off

Removing Barriers to Disengagement

Managers can impact these barriers to engagement in many ways. All involve knowing your team members and communicating on a regular basis.

Unfulfilled Expectations – Why it's a problem: The term "psychological contract" can be defined as what you expect in return for what you provide at work. When employees join your organization there is an expectation that they will receive certain things. They may expect the work environment and resources provided to be similar to what they had at a prior organization, or they may hope they are not! Employees create an image in their mind of what they expect, but they don't always verbalize it, assuming their image will be reality.

Sometimes we don't even realize how important our expectations are to our satisfaction. Only when we are disappointed do we realize how important one of our expectations is to us. A failure to have expectations satisfied can feel like a broken promise. It can be as simple as "I never worked downtown before, and I didn't know I would have to pay for parking" to "I didn't know I was going to be evaluated on teamwork" to "No one ever said that this is an exempt position and I wouldn't receive overtime pay." When expectations are not understood and assumptions are made, disappointment always follows.

Unfulfilled Expectations – What managers can do: Managers have two specific strategies for managing engagement in this area: Realistic job previews (RJP) and onboarding, both of which were discussed in the "All Aboard!" chapter. During your RJP you are allowing the candidate to opt out of accepting a job that he or she knows won't be engaging. During onboarding you are communicating what the organization expects so there won't be a misunderstanding later. During my time as human resources director one of the worst things I heard team members say was, "I didn't know, no one told me." This engagement barrier is such an easy fix...just tell them!

Organizational Changes – Why it's a problem: When a change occurs, it is human nature to first look at how the change will have a personal negative impact. How many times have you heard children exclaim "that's not fair" when hearing something they don't like? As adults, we no longer yell "that's not fair" when change occurs, but our inner child might be screaming it in our heads. People will consciously or unconsciously change their behavior to bring equity/fairness back in their world. They are constantly weighing their efforts against what they are getting to see if it's fair. If a team member decides he or she doesn't like the change it may cause disengagement, and if left to fester, the issue may lead to his or her resignation.

Organizational Changes – What managers can do: Managers are the change agents in their organizations. The amount of disruption change causes can be directly linked to how the change agent announced and implemented the change. Experienced managers are change agents who immediately seek out all the information they can about the change so they can explain to the team the who, what, when, where, how, and why of the change. They know they're the catalyst of success. They look at the "why" of change from the organization's perspective; this is the driving force of the change. Managers also look at the restraining forces that may interfere with the successful implementation of the change. Use your empathy skills and develop answers around these questions:

- Why is the change necessary; what is driving the change?
- How does the change negatively impact my team members? Would some team members be impacted more than others?
- How does the change positively impact my team members? What are the positive impact items that I can share with my team?
- In what ways can I assist my team members in adapting to this change?
- What barriers exist to our successfully adapting to this change?
- How can I enlist my team members' help in removing the restraining forces of change through involvement and problem solving?

Demonstration of a Change Agent in Action

Linda, a customer service manager, learns that the company has signed a new client that will increase her department's workload by 20 percent. Due to budgetary constraints, she can't hire any additional staff to handle the increase. She realizes this change may have the potential to impact the engagement of her team members.

Linda decides to hold a meeting with her team members and give them the positive impacts of the change first: 1) After a renewed sales and marketing effort, the company has successfully signed its first new client in a year. 2) The company anticipates the new client will contribute to the reputation of the company and attract even more new clients. Linda knows it is critical that every department demonstrate a level of outstanding service, so she locates all the details her team will need about the new client.

Linda understands that communication, honesty, and transparency are critical when developing trust that leads to engagement, so she also shares the "not so good" news with her team. The company will not realize the additional revenue from this client for quite a while, so no department will be able to add additional staff, at least in the short run. She lets team members know that she recognizes that this change will be quite a challenge for them to absorb the extra workload, and she needs their help to achieve this goal.

To gain input and involvement from her team, for one week Linda posts an idea board in the department for team members to contribute their ideas on how to handle the increased workload. As people stop by and see the ideas, they think of other ideas and add them. Also during this week, she encourages her team members to meet with her one-on-one to share their concerns privately. At the end of the week, she holds a problem-solving meeting where the team discusses the merits of each idea, considers new ideas, and creates an action plan. By the time the new client is on board, the team is fully committed and engaged in its successful transition. The situation has gone from a change the company has forced on the team members to a transition plan they own.

Personal Circumstances – Why it's a problem: We hire whole people with lives outside of work, not just a person with skills we need for the company. Most people say it's important to keep your personal life and work life separate; however, when a personal problem becomes so severe or lasts a long period of time, keeping emotions in check at work becomes more and more difficult. Productivity in the form of quality and quantity may suffer as part of your team member's brain stays focused on their personal situation. The team member may reach a "boiling point" one day and have a conflict with a customer or coworker, or may resign from feeling overwhelmed by their personal circumstance.

Personal Circumstances – What managers can do: This engagement barrier is the hardest for a manager to impact, but there are actions managers can take even in this area. Experienced managers know their team members, including their typical on-the-job behavior. When they notice changes, they don't wait or ignore their observations, they find out the "why" behind the change in behavior. After probing for things in the work environment that might impact the behavior change, managers might learn that a personal problem is the cause and that the team member may or may not want to talk about it. Many people are very private and don't wish to share this information, in which case managers should respect their privacy and not intrude. A good strategy, if this is the case, is to refer them to the human resources department or, if the company has one, an employee assistance program (EAP). Community resources may also be able to assist your team members in managing their personal circumstances, and they will be glad the company has cared enough about them as an individual to offer this referral. If your team member freely discusses his/her changed personal situation, determine if the company can accommodate their situation with a leave of absence, a change in work hours, or a transfer to a different position.

> *"Employees who believe that management is concerned about them as a whole person – not just an employee – are more productive, more satisfied, more fulfilled. Satisfied employees mean satisfied customers, which leads to profitability."*
>
> ~Anne M. Mulchahy, former CEO of Xerox

Measuring Engagement

What people think and feel about the organization, its leaders, and their co-workers impacts how engaged they are at work. We can see how their thoughts and feelings translate to behavior by the initiative they take, suggestions they make, the extra effort they use, and their persistence in solving problems. But we never really know how people think and feel until we ask. Organizations determine engagement with the organization and with the manager by surveys, focus groups, or one-on-one conversations.

Engagement with the Organization measures how engaged employees are with the organization as a whole, and by extension, how they feel about senior management. This factor has to do with confidence in organizational leadership as well as trust, fairness, values, and respect such as how people treat them, both at work and outside of work.

Engagement with My Manager is a more specific measure of how employees feel about their direct supervisors. Topics include feeling valued, being treated fairly, receiving feedback and direction, and generally, having a strong working relationship between the employee and manager based on mutual respect.

What is almost as important as asking for feedback is providing participants with the results of the survey. Team members must see action taken as a result of their time and effort in completing the survey, or they won't bother to respond in the future.

One mistake organizations make is surveying too often, since it takes time to analyze the survey results and present action plans. Doing an excellent job of collecting information, creating action plans, and involving team members in creating improvement is better than surveying frequently and letting the results just sit there. Team members will be more willing to provide feedback if they know something will actually be done to make improvements. They also will be more willing to answer a survey if they don't feel "surveyed to death" with too many surveys.

Employee Retention—How to Keep People on the Bus

How do you know when someone is thinking about leaving your organization? I asked this question to a training class one day, and one of the answers I received was "when the pictures of the family disappear from their workstation." After we had a good laugh at this response, we discussed the fact that if the family disappeared, the employee has already made the decision to leave and there probably was no way to save the situation. The team member's heart and mind had already left the building, and very soon his/her body was going to follow.

A proactive engagement step is to identify the key contributors in your department—those who make a difference in the organization. This group may include so-called "high potential" employees who are projected to be promoted to the next level or levels of the organization. Key contributors are those team members who, if they left, would feel like a big loss. They quite often are the unsung heroes that customers never see but who provide a valuable service to those who do serve the customer. Consider this question: "If the CEO and the janitor both stopped coming to work for two weeks, who would you miss most?" Many people would say the janitor!

Our local breakfast restaurant lost its egg cook, who had worked there for more than 20 years. Although the restaurant immediately hired a replacement, it quickly found out the cook was not easily replaceable because of the amount of knowledge and speed he had developed over the years. The impact was that service slowed down, resulting in long wait times and some customers giving up and walking out. Who would you miss in your organization if they left tomorrow? Do you take some team members for granted, assuming they would always be there? Do they feel "taken for granted?" Do you have a janitor or egg-cook type employee who you will discover is a critical team member only when they leave?

Literally more than a million job search websites exist. Is one of your key employees searching right now? Is there something occurring in your organization that might lead your employees to start looking?

A few triggers that might lead your key players to think about leaving include downsizing, reorganization, reduction in stock price, merger or acquisition, and industry downturn. Are any of these factors true for your organization right now?

The Bad News: Losing a high performer is disruptive and costly in terms of productivity, business disruption, and customer service. Your key players may even take other good employees and customers with them to their new companies. The Good News: Managers are the secret weapon in combating turnover. Team members are frequently more committed to their organization because of the actions taken by their manager to build a strong professional relationship. Managers impact engagement by being available to their teams; treating employees with respect; communicating company goals; informing employees of job performance; and providing constructive feedback, coaching, and recognition.

> *"If you are lucky enough to be someone's employer,
> then you have a moral obligation to make sure
> people do look forward to coming to work in the
> morning."*
>
> ~John Macky, Whole Foods Market

Here are a few tips for improving retention in your organization:

- **Identify Early Warning Signs** – Signs may include a drop in productivity, loss of enthusiasm, withdrawal from the team, and an increase in time off. Managers who know their employees will be able to identify changes in behavior that may indicate a key player is looking outside of the company and take action early enough to prevent the key player from leaving. Don't wait until the family pictures have left the building.

- **Recognize and Celebrate Success** – People enjoy having a sense of achievement and feeling like winners. Managers have the ability to create a climate where success breeds success and people feel recognized and appreciated for their individual and team accomplishments in customized, targeted ways that fit their preferences. Why would anyone want to leave a winning team?

- **Get to Know Your Employees as Individuals** – Find out your employees' motivations and strengths. Learn what gets them excited about coming to work and the type of tasks they enjoy. Also find out what interests them off the job such as hobbies, interests, and family so they know they are seen as whole people and not just as employees.

- **Discuss Advancement and Development** – People may leave an organization if they don't clearly see what's next for them. They may also leave if they like their current position but don't feel they are growing in it. Managers can learn the individual goals for each of their key team members and assist in their achievement by encouraging enrollment in training programs, helping them market themselves internally, offering challenging assignments, and more. See Chapter 7, "Create a Map for Others" for career discussion ideas.

- **Create Line of Sight to Outcomes** – Employees need to know not only the company vision but also how it is related to their specific job. They need to know the job they do is critical and the impact to the organization and the rest of the team when they aren't there or perform to expectations. One of the best illustrations of this concept is the story of when Present Kennedy visited NASA in 1962. The story I've heard is that when he introduced himself to a janitor carrying a broom and asked him what he was doing, the man replied: "Well, Mr. President, I'm helping to put a man on the moon." To create that type of vision connection with your team members, meet with them regularly and ask questions such as: Does your work make a difference? Do you feel fully utilized in your role? What do you need to feel more successful at work? How can I assist you?

- **Assess Engagement** – An engagement assessment helps to direct your focus toward specific areas of strengths and weaknesses in your culture. Involving your team members in action planning as a result of the survey furthers the engagement of your team.

"Imagine if your company doubled the number of great managers and engaged employees. Gallup finds that the 30 million engaged employees in the U.S. come up with most of the innovative ideas, create most of a company's new customers, and have the most entrepreneurial energy."

~Jim Clifton, Chairman and CEO of Gallup, from *State of the American Workplace*

Summary

Engaged employees make a major impact on company results. Your team members may fall within three categories: engaged, not engaged, or disengaged. Managers can proactively remove barriers to engagement within three areas: unfulfilled expectations, organizational changes, and personal circumstances. Retaining your key team members is an important role of an experienced manager. Tips for improving retention include identify early warning signs, recognize and celebrate success, get to know your employees as individuals, discuss advancement and development, create line of sight to outcomes, and assess engagement. By identifying critical members of your team and applying an engagement strategy, experienced managers can keep the right people on the bus and committed to the journey of the organization.

Building Your Map
Follow-up Activities

1. **Think about your current team and determine the percentage engaged, not engaged, and actively disengaged.**

2. **Make a list of behaviors you've seen in each of these categories to assist you in recognizing them in your team members**
   - ❏ Engaged _____
   - ❏ Not Engaged _____
   - ❏ Disengaged _____

3. **Identify one critical team member in the engaged category.** Have a discussion to let the person know how critical they are and ask what engages them at work.

4. **Identify one critical team member in the not engaged category.** Have a discussion to let the person know how critical they are and ask what barriers can be removed so they can become more engaged at work.

5. **Think about an upcoming change that would impact the engagement of your team.** Create a plan to open lines of communication, gain trust, and encourage involvement.

Where to Go From Here
Helpful Training Topics

- ❑ Vital Learning's workshop, "Retaining Winning Talent"
- ❑ Communication skills
- ❑ Facilitation skills
- ❑ Leading change

SEVEN

CREATE A MAP FOR OTHERS...
Career Planning for Your Team

Chapter Learning Points
- Hold career planning discussions
- Understand steps for succession planning

> *"Always define WHAT you want to do with your life and WHAT you have to offer to the world, in terms of your favorite talents/gifts/skills—not in terms of a job title."*
>
> ~ Richard N. Bolles, author of *What Color Is Your Parachute?*

You Are Here

How do you navigate when visiting a new shopping mall for the first time? To help visitors navigate, a mall will put up store directories located throughout the space. I'm sure everyone has at least seen these types of maps, and many of us know their value and use them regularly. Mall directories usually have a list of stores by category and a pictorial map showing store locations—and of course the whereabouts of the food court.

One critical item to notice is that not only do these store directories reveal the locations of places where you want to go; they also contain an X or circle labeled, "you are here." Obviously, it is difficult to navigate to a store's location unless you know the starting point of your journey. By knowing your starting point you can determine the best route to take you there, how far you have to walk to get there, and the other stores that might interest you along the way.

Now picture the largest mall in the US: the Mall of America in Bloomington, Minnesota. This mall is so large it could fit 32 Boeing 747's inside, and it contains over 500 stores. This mall probably doubles or triples your normal choices of stores to visit. Navigating through this mall is more complex and will take longer with probably several stops along the way to figure out where you are as you consult more of the "you are here" signs. The sheer number of stores provides more diversity of choice as well. You may have intended to visit your favorite store and instead start noticing several new stores that fit your interests.

So what does all this shopping discussion have to do with career planning? Part of a manager's job is to help provide the map for employees, to assist them in preparing for future jobs that fit their interests, to provide them advice on how to get there, and, most importantly, identify employees' "you are here" map based on their current experience, skills, and abilities. Smaller companies may have fewer career choices while larger companies may be harder to navigate, much like the Mall of America.

Fear Around Career Discussions

Organizations that conduct climate or engagement surveys report a typical area of complaint is that employees want more opportunities to advance their careers and the ability to clearly see paths to career progression. Employees don't typically initiate career discussions with their managers. Some aren't sure how to approach their manager, and others fear that their manager will see them as disloyal if they express interest in other jobs in the company. Still others draw their own conclusions about a lack of advancement by observing how job-posting programs are administered and how many people are hired for higher-level positions from outside of the organization.

Managers may have several concerns about career conversations as well, including:

- Fear of telling the employee there aren't any openings right now for promotion.
- Fear of losing their most productive employee to another department.
- Fear of not having the budget to offer employees training and development opportunities.
- Fear if they bring up career planning, they might be setting expectations that they can't deliver.
- Fear that if they discuss careers with employees who don't want a promotion, it may cause them discomfort.
- Fear that employees will have lofty career goals that don't match their skills and abilities, which can lead to the fear of having to tell the employee they aren't qualified.

- Fear that employees will expect you as their manager to assume total responsibility for their career and training.

What is the result of all this fear? Career conversations are avoided and simply don't get done. This chapter will provide managers with the confidence, competence, and courage to have those important career conversations with their team members.

The New Definition of Careers

In the past, people talked about climbing the ladder of success. The whole idea was you started at the bottom rung of the ladder and, step by step, you received promotions to the next level. Careers today, however, mimic an elevator that may stop floor by floor along the way or may take the express route right to the top. Career elevators may have employees making needed stops to gain experience before arriving at the "floor" of their choice. Careers may also be like the moving sidewalks you see in some airports that move people on the same level from area to area before getting them to the point of taking an elevator upwards.

Considering this new definition of careers is important because it assists managers to hold career discussions and overcome some of the fears associated with them. Managers need to create a new definition of the term career, one that reflects what employees want. Not everyone wants to climb the ladder of success or get on the career elevator. Some employees are happy on the moving sidewalk gaining experience along the way laterally.

In the next several paragraphs, we discuss examples of how career goals may differ by person.

Doris is employed in her perfect job, which is a terrific match to her skills and interests. She does not have an interest in any other position, but she still wants career development. Doris isn't worried about titles; her idea of a career discussion would revolve around how she could continue to develop her skills in her current role in order to become the best in her field and a major contributor of new ideas for the organization.

Maria very much wants to climb the ladder of success. She is currently in the field she loves in an entry-level position. She wants to gain more responsibility and develop her leadership skills so she can be promoted to a supervisor and then a manager, who knows...maybe a vice president. Maria is an enthusiastic learner who regularly volunteers for assignments that will allow her to grow and expand her knowledge.

Stu is thinking about retirement. He's had a successful career and wants to get off the elevator. He has extensive experience and sees career development as something he can help do for others through mentoring and special projects.

Julio wasn't sure what profession he wanted to work in after college and now feels he chose the wrong one. His idea of career development is assistance in developing a plan on how he can gain the skills and experience to make the transition to his new chosen field.

Sharon just had her second child; her first is only two years old. Balancing her family and work responsibilities are challenging for her right now. She worries that when she leaves promptly at 5:00 pm every day to pick up her children from day care, she is giving the impression she isn't committed to her career, which isn't true.

We just read about five different employees who require five different types of career discussions. As their manager, how do you flex your strategy so all of your employees feel like they have the opportunity to advance their career and the ability to clearly see paths to career progression? It's a simple answer...ask them!

Simple Steps for Career Discussions

In Chapter 3, "Getting to Know Your Traveling Companions" of *TMM*, you learned the importance of the Getting-To-Know-You meeting. The Getting-to-Know-You questions from this chapter are:

1. What is your preferred style at work?
2. What form of communication do you prefer?
3. How do you like to be recognized?
4. What do you like about the job you do? What do you dislike? What can be changed?
5. What do you like and dislike about the work environment? What can be changed?
6. What are your future goals, and how can I help you achieve them? What additional training do you need?
7. Is there anything else you want me, as your manager, to know about you?

This career planning meeting is a way to find out your employee's expectations and preferences and build trust and open communications. Your first meeting with your employee should have contained all seven questions. During subsequent meetings you may have skipped a few questions or just asked if anything has changed since the last time you spoke. In question six you asked, "What are your future goals and what additional training would you like?" Although it isn't labeled as such, this question is related to career planning. Keep asking this question and you are on your way to helping your employees manage their careers and increasing engagement in your environment.

Again using our mall directory example, the answer to question six will reveal where your employees want to go, but you will also need information for the "you are here" part of career development. An experienced manager can make all the difference during this part of the discussion.

Employees who receive in-depth feedback during the performance management process already have information about their current skills and abilities. As an effective manager, you have complimented and reinforced strengths and also created employee accountability to work on development needs.

Combining previous feedback with the desired destination you learned during your career discussion, you and your employees can create a path of success. Let's revisit our five employees to demonstrate how you can make this connection.

Doris' "you are here" – Doris already has a high level of skills and abilities in her field, including an advanced degree. **Her plan**: After hearing her goals, you suggest she joins a professional networking group to hear about best practices she might want to emulate, and attend professional development conferences in her field. The information she hears will give her an opportunity to suggest and implement creative new ideas.

Marie's "you are here" – Marie is enthusiastic and learns quickly, but she still has a lot to learn before assuming a new role. **Her plan:** Marie will locate the job description, which contains a list of job duties and required competencies, for the next role she would like to assume. The two of you can use this as a guide, examining each job duty listed and determine what she has to do to get the experience or education she will need to be successful. This process is also known as a "gap analysis."

Stu's "you are here" – Stu has an excellent track record of achieving results for the organization and has the interpersonal skills to be a mentor. **His plan:** You will immediately start relying on him to assist in on-boarding new members of the team. He will also consider whether he wants to change jobs to work full time in a training position, and, if yes, obtain that job description for a gap analysis.

Julio's "you are here" – Julio's performance has been acceptable and he is skilled in his current field. Moving to a new field will require either a lateral move or a step down to gain the experience he'll need. In other words, he might need to press the down button on the elevator and spend time on a different floor for a while. He may also need to return to school to complete a different degree program. **His plan:** To assist Julio in learning more about the expectations of his newly identified field, and to obtain advice on how he can start planning his development, you set up a meeting for him with an executive in that area.

Sharon's "you are here" – Sharon has shown the ability to assume higher-level responsibilities. She tells you she will be in a better position personally next year to start working on her career. **Her plan:** Find out more about what positions she might be interested in for the future and then look for opportunities where she can start developing the skills in her current job without taking on additional tasks or training right now, which would require working hours after 5:00 pm. She gets on the moving sidewalk career option, picking up skills and insights until she is ready to take the elevator up a level.

"A good manager is a man who isn't worried about his own career but rather the careers of those who work for him."

~ H. S. M. Burns, past president Shell Oil Company

When you spend the time to demonstrate your interest in your employee's careers, their engagement at work will increase, and, in turn, improve results for your department.

Development Options

Just as there is a new definition of the concept of career, there is also a new definition for development. Development used to mean "send them to a training class." A training class may not always be the right answer or the affordable option, though. A training class may not be available that meets the specific training needs or learning style of your employee, or maybe your training budget has been cut. Maybe you've sent employees to a training class but change hasn't occurred, or they did not develop the skills promised.

Now is the time to think creatively! Let's look at one of our employees, Maria, and her desire to eventually lead a group of people. You could simply send her to a leadership class, or instead she can explore other options. For example:

1. Read books on leadership. There are over 150,000 leadership books are available on Amazon.com.
2. Watch videos on leadership. At least 3,000,000 exist on YouTube.com.
3. Read articles on leadership. Enter "leadership articles" on Google.com and you will receive over 97,000,000 results.
4. Create a report or presentation on what she learned from any of the first three suggestions.
5. Lead a team at work in a special project, then describe what she learned about her leadership skills.
6. Interview leaders she admires, asking the question: "What skills do great leaders possess?"
7. Volunteer in a leadership role in a nonprofit or professional association.

8. Locate a leadership assessment to get feedback and suggestions for improvement. One I like to recommend is *Work of Leaders* by Wiley Publishing.
9. Locate a leader mentor who is willing to meet with Maria on a regular basis to provide an impartial sounding board.

I'm sure you can probably think of even more ideas to add to this list. The best option for development depends heavily on how your employees like to learn. They should participate in not only what needs to be learned but also how to learn the skills identified in their gap analysis.

> *"Knowledge is power. You can't be in a career, for that matter even a relationship, unless you know everything there is to know about it."*
>
> ~Randeep Hooda, Indian film actor

Succession Planning

Managers need to look at career planning from two sides:

1. Your employees' career interests
2. What talent your organization needs in the future

We've already learned how to discuss your employee's career interests. Now it's time to turn our attention to succession planning, which entails identifying those employees who have the right skills to meet the future challenges facing your organization.

Organizations have a choice when it comes to promotions: hire from outside the organization or promote from within. Both strategies have advantages and disadvantages. You will face times when you need critical, specialized experience for an opening that just doesn't exist internally and there isn't time to develop it. Then you may need to recruit the expertise from outside your organization. At other times, there will be competitive advantage to promote employees from within the organization, for their critical knowledge of the inner workings of the company and its culture.

What do you think happens to organizations that only hire people from outside and don't promote from within? The talented employees who want to be promoted will get frustrated and leave if they feel that is the only way to get ahead in their careers, and you lose the opportunity to develop and promote people who already understand your industry and culture.

> *"Ten of eleven good-to-great CEOs came from inside the company."*
>
> ~ Jim Collins, author *Good to Great*

Your role in succession planning will depend on your management position or level. You may be involved in participating in succession planning by identifying talented employees who could succeed current incumbents or you may be identified as a backup candidate yourself. Regardless, as an experienced manager you should have at least general knowledge of the purpose and process of succession planning.

The first step in succession planning is to identify key critical positions in your organization, typically in leadership roles. They are critical because leaving them open for an extended period of time would be detrimental to your business.

The next step is to identify who in your organization is currently ready to replace these key positions and who could be ready with further development, noting what development they need.

Here is a succession planning example: A small manufacturing company identifies the vice president of manufacturing as one of its critical positions. David, who is doing an outstanding job and has no plans to leave the company, holds that position, but that is not the point in succession planning. The point is to ask *if* David left the organization *who* has the skills and experience to replace him? The answer to that question is either Larry, one of the current engineering managers, or Sara, one of the current production managers. You also identify what skills each person needs to develop to be successful when and if the time comes to replace David. You determine Larry needs to develop his leadership skills and Sara should finish her business degree and develop her analytical skills.

What if David never leaves. Have you wasted your employees' time? No, because you have taken an interest in each person's career and provided developmental opportunities for their growth. But if David does leave someday, your company is in the position to have a seamless transition with an internal promotion.

Organizations succeed by having the right people in the right places at the right times. The implementation of an effective career planning process will help to ensure that your organization is prepared for future success.

Summary

A new definition exists of a career that doesn't just fit the traditional "climbing the ladder of success." Employees can use new methods for gaining knowledge in addition to attending training classes. Experienced managers overcome their fear of career planning by developing skills in two processes: 1) conducting effective performance reviews to give team members feedback on "where they are now" and 2) holding career discussions with questions to determine "where they want to go." Managers then can hold brainstorming sessions with their employees on how to plan a path to get from here to there.

Building Your Map
Follow-up Activities

1. List your concerns about holding career discussions with your team members.
   - ❏ _____
   - ❏ _____
   - ❏ _____

2. Create a schedule to complete Getting-to-Know-You meetings with your team members.

3. Determine if your organization has career planning resources.

4. Determine if you have a training and development budget.

5. **Think about a typical development need that might be discussed during your career planning discussions.** Brainstorm at least four creative ways to develop that skill in addition to attending a training class.
   - ❏ _____
   - ❏ _____
   - ❏ _____
   - ❏ _____

6. **Hold career-planning discussions with your team members.** Use the mall directory metaphor in your discussions.

Where to Go From Here
Helpful Training Topics

- ❏ Career planning
- ❏ Communication skills
- ❏ Brainstorming skills
- ❏ Coaching skills

EIGHT

THE ROAD TO EXCELLENCE
Managing Employee Performance

Chapter Learning Points
- Evaluate team member performance
- Create positive performance improvement plans

> *"Excellence is a continuous process and not an accident."*
> ~A. P. J. Abdul Kalam, former president of India

Keeping Performance on the Road to Excellence

What do you do when you become lost on a journey? Pull over and consult your map or GPS? Stop and ask for directions? Do you seek directions as soon as you realize you are going the wrong direction, or do you wander around aimlessly for an hour? The price of delay means that you will probably be late for an important event. If you are on the way to an airport, you might miss your flight and a long-awaited vacation.

When you solve a problem at work, do you admit you need assistance and seek advice, or struggle along while others are wondering what is wrong? How about your employees? Do they always seek out help?

The key is to solve the problem as soon as possible. As soon as you know where you went wrong, you can get back on the path to your destination. As soon as you know your employees are off their path of success, you should provide them with the feedback needed to keep performance on the right path.

Many managers postpone giving feedback when they realize employees are going down the wrong path. The wrong path represents a failure to meet behavior expectations or performance goals. By postponing feedback, these managers are paying the price of delay. The price of delay includes:

- The problem continues or gets worse.
- Behavior becomes contagious and other employees start to copy it.
- Behavior becomes a habit, which is harder to stop.
- Customers are affected by quality issues or delays in service.
- Team members become frustrated if part of their evaluation includes team performance.
- You develop a reputation of being a manager who allows problems to fester.

Managing performance works best when it emphasizes the day-to-day process of communicating expectations and providing feedback. Why pay the price of delay when you can provide feedback early and often and have a high-performing, engaged team that achieves results?

Here are a few ideas to develop a high-achievement management style that will result in greater goal accomplishments for your team:

- **Establish Expectations** – When team members don't know the "rules of the game" they become frustrated. The rules are your expectations. One of the worst things to hear is "I didn't know, no one told me." Provide clear expectations of behavior and performance including a review of the job description.

- **Set High But Achievable Goals** – Keep team members focused on the "bottom line" by establishing challenging but achievable goals. Involve team members in the goal-setting process for greater commitment.

- **Coach and Give Feedback** – Encourage your team members to be "the best they can be" by looking for "coachable moments." Give both positive and corrective feedback based on the expectations established and goals set.

- **Remove Barriers to Success** – Are there processes, policies, or systems that slow down your team members? Remove or streamline barriers so your team members feel successful and supported to always work efficiently.

High-achievement managers keep their team members focused on the path to performance—all rowing in the right direction to achieve their goals. Managers maintain this focus through effective performance management.

Performance Management

According to the University of California, Berkley, performance management is defined as "an ongoing process of communication between a supervisor and an employee that occurs throughout the year, in support of accomplishing the strategic objectives of the organization. The communication process includes clarifying expectations, setting objectives, identifying goals, providing feedback, and reviewing results."

Unfortunately, some managers see performance management as the once-a-year performance appraisal form they complete. Performance reviews can be anxiety producing for both managers and employees. Managers dislike the amount of time it takes and have a fear of possible confrontation. Employees worry about being surprised during discussions and are unclear about what is expected of them.

Effective, experienced managers view performance reviews as an ongoing communication process. They reap the benefits that managing individual employee performance has in achieving the goals for their departments. When done correctly, performance evaluations provide motivational value through open and honest communication, and they serve to keep the organization focused on achieving its goals.

Every organization has its own method of performance feedback, and many use a standardized online or paper form. Learning your company's philosophy, processes, and forms is important. You may wish to have a copy of the form and other review instructions in front of you as you read the rest of this chapter.

Here is a general performance management process that works with just about any performance review program:

1. Establish goals and expectations
2. Observe, track progress, and capture data
3. Provide ongoing coaching and direction
4. Complete your company's forms
5. Discuss the performance review

1. Establish Goals and Expectations

Many managers skip this important step in performance management, but experienced managers know that investing in the front end of the process reaps the greatest dividends later in not only achieving goals but creating a motivational environment for their team members.

Expectations provide a framework of how to perform a job. To achieve high expectations, setting goals, which are the measurable end result of performance, is important. Clear expectations ensure that employees know what's expected, how to achieve results, and how to monitor their own performance. Setting expectations should include a review of job duties and required competencies. Goals set at the beginning of the review period can be measured at the end to determine results achieved.

> *"In business, the idea of measuring what you are doing, picking the measurements that count like customer satisfaction and performance...you thrive on that."*
>
> ~Bill Gates, founder of Microsoft, inventor, and philanthropist

Many performance review forms contain a section for goal setting. This is sometimes referred to as management by objectives (MBO), which is a process where the manager and employee jointly agree on goals for the year and how to achieve them.

A goal is a future target of accomplishment usually requiring some effort to achieve. Individuals should be shown a connection between their performance and department/company goals. It is important to distinguish between a goal and regular job responsibility. For example, consider an accounts payable clerk position. A regular job responsibility for this position is to correctly pay invoices on time. A goal for this position might be to create a tracking system to calculate the average length of time to pay invoices.

Since we are discussing goals, now would be a good time to review Chapter 5, "Setting Your Course and Speed" from *TMM*. This chapter introduces the five steps of goal setting: 1) Goal, 2) Resources, 3) Plan, 4) Milestones, and 5) Measurements. Using the five steps of goal setting ensures you actually set achievable goals and not just "wish" for results.

What do you think of the following statement and does it use all five steps? *"Someday I will dive the Great Barrier Reef in Australia."* In the example, the resources, a plan on how to achieve it, and the milestones are not identified. The measurement of achievement is whether you actually get to dive the reef, but as my friend and fellow management consultant Carl Youngberg likes to say, "Someday is not a day of the week!"

"Connect the dots between individual roles and the goals of the organization. When people see that connection, they get a lot of energy out of work. They feel the importance, dignity, and meaning in their job."

~Ken Blanchard and Scott Blanchard, "Do Your People Really Know What You Expect From Them?" Fast Company

---

Many organizations use a graphic rating scale performance review form with categories such as: quality, quantity, teamwork, initiative, customer service, and more. Describing performance levels based on your rating system will define the expectations of on-the-job behaviors that result in goal achievement. Let's say one of your company's performance rating categories is teamwork, and your review system has four rating levels. Providing a description of observable behaviors in each rating level not only assists you when it's time to complete the appraisal, but it also sets clear expectations for your team members. Here are examples of behavior in each rating level for the category of teamwork:

- **Superior** – Regularly makes suggestions to improve teamwork among coworkers, and is the first to offer assistance to others.
- **Fully Satisfactory** – Takes the initiative to provide assistance to coworkers when own work is completed.
- **Needs Improvement** – Waits for someone to ask for help before assisting others.
- **Unacceptable** – Does not assist coworkers and avoids opportunities to interact with them.

The more you can specifically tie the descriptions to the actual job, the more meaningful it will be to your team members.

2. Observe, Track Progress, and Capture Data

Reviews become a more accurate reflection of performance and are easier to complete if managers use a tracking mechanism throughout the review period to capture significant events and data. Tracking can be electronic or on paper. Significant events can include:

- Internal and external customer compliments or complaints
- Employee suggestions and contributions
- Results of coaching sessions
- Formal discipline discussions
- Participation on task forces
- Providing assistance to coworkers, such as training new employees
- Completion of special projects
- Quantity statistics
- Training programs attended
- Goals and results achieved

Documentation provides the basis for ongoing coaching and assists you in accurately completing the annual performance review. Documentation should be objective and include examples of performance strengths as well as areas needing improvement.

One approach is for managers to create a page for every employee to capture what are called "critical incidents." Managers can develop a habit to always record significant events throughout the year on the employee's specific page to assist in completing their review. Both positive and improvement-needed comments are recorded with dates, typically by dividing the page in half.

3. Supply Coaching and Direction

Never wait until the performance review to give feedback. The review should merely be a summary of results and discussions. Remember the phrase: *"Nothing new on the performance review."*

The best managers share the philosophy, "I want my employees to the best they can be." If you truly want your employees to live up to their potential, you will never hesitate to provide timely feedback. Feedback is like holding a mirror up for reflection, sharing observations about your team members' performance or behaviors on the job. It is important to provide feedback as soon as possible. For example, think about driving down the road and noticing your car is veering to the left. Isn't it better to immediately correct your steering to direct your car back into your lane rather than wait until another car comes along, causing an accident?

Don't wait for your team members' performance problems to become severe before providing course corrections. In addition to observing off-track performance, your job as a manager is also to point out when you observe excellence, so the team member can repeat the behavior.

Feedback should be provided in a coaching setting that facilitates problem solving and resolution. After you point out your observations, involve the employee in a dialog regarding how to either continue or change behavior. If you follow the advice of *"Nothing new on the performance review,"* you don't want to be in the position of explaining a performance deficiency for the first time during your review discussion and have the employee say, *"Why didn't you tell me before?"*

4. Complete Your Company's Appraisal Forms

If you have done a good job in the first three steps of performance management, step four becomes very easy. It is merely a summary document of everything that happened during the review period.

In addition to providing a rating for performance categories and an update on goal accomplishments, many organizations provide a place for written comments. Comments on appraisals should be objective and not subjective. They must be completely unbiased. Objective statements are verifiable by facts or quantitative statistics. Subjective statements are based on an opinion or conclusion by the appraiser and, therefore, may be perceived as unfair or biased.

Here are a few examples:

Subjective	Objective
• Lacks customer empathy	• Does not use eye contact
• Doesn't care about the job	• Absent ten days
• Is careless	• Error rate is 25%
• Disorganized	• Project deadline missed

For performance comments to be effective, they must be:

- **Clear** – Readily understood, short, and to the point

- **Specific** – Utilizing dates, numbers, and descriptive instances

- **Business Focused** – Discussing the impact to the company and/or coworkers

- **Self-Esteem Focused** – Treating employees as responsible adults and preserving their self-esteem and your relationship

- And of course **Non-Discriminatory**!

5. Discuss the Performance Review

You have written the review form, but the performance management process is not complete until there is a dialog between the manager and the team member. The performance appraisal shouldn't be something that is done "to" the employee but something that includes the employee. Just as some students believe that they earn grades and others believe grades are just given by the teacher, team members need to feel the review isn't just "given" but a reflection of what has actually occurred throughout the review period. This is a good time for team members to discuss what they think about their performance during the review period, and their plans for development for the future.

Give team members advance notice to prepare for the meeting. Explain that the purpose of the discussion is to review past work in order to improve future performance, satisfaction, and personal development. Then ask team members to discuss their performance and how it has changed from the last review period. If specific goals were established, ask for the results from the employee's perspective.

Now it is the manager's turn to discuss what was documented on the review form. Give credit and praise for what team members have accomplished. Discuss what was not accomplished and ask the team member for suggestions on how to solve developmental issues. Keep the discussion future oriented and not focused on the past, which can't be changed. The team member should leave the meeting feeling inspired to reach for excellence during the next review cycle.

> *"The best way to inspire people to superior performance is to convince them by everything you do and by your everyday attitude that you are wholeheartedly supporting them."*
>
> ~Harold S. Geneen, former president of ITT

Employee Self-Appraisals

Some organizations use an employee self-appraisal form. The form may look exactly like the form the manager uses or something similar. It typically contains a section for the team member to list the goals achieved during the past year and a place to rate the behaviors required for the position. The purpose of the self-appraisal is to make performance management more of a partnership than just a one-way judgment by the manager, which demonstrates trust and respect for the employee's opinion and facilitates open dialogue.

Managers are sometimes reluctant to use self-appraisals, believing that team members will over inflate their evaluations which might lead to conflict if the manager's rating is lower than the employee's rating. Of course this does happen, but team members may believe they aren't being evaluated high enough even if there isn't a formal form to fill out. The form helps to pinpoint areas of disagreement, which can lead to meaningful dialogue of expectations and note where the employee is falling short. What many managers actually experience is that team members actually are harder on themselves in their own ratings.

Time to Start the Process Over

Congratulations, you've successfully managed the performance review process! Because performance management is a cycle, it is ongoing. Now it's time to start again for the next review period by setting goals to evaluate next year.

Summary

The phrase "Nothing new on the performance review" is a good reminder that performance management is an ongoing communication and feedback process. The process starts with establishing goals and expectations, and then performance is tracked throughout the review period followed by coaching. Follow your company's performance appraisal process and properly use its forms, including a self-appraisal form if applicable. The process is not complete until managers hold an open dialog with team members to include their perspective of their own performance.

Building Your Map
Follow-up Activities

1. **Describe your organization's review process.**
   - ❑ Is there a specific form to complete?
   - ❑ How many rating levels are there? What are they?
   - ❑ Does your form have evaluation categories? What are they?
   - ❑ Are there specific instructions for managers on how to complete the process?
   - ❑ Does your organization utilize a self-appraisal form?

2. **Describe how you will track performance throughout the review period.**

3. **Provide feedback.** Choose a team member and practice providing feedback. Remember the purpose of providing feedback is so your employees can "be the best they can be."

4. **Practice writing review comments.** Choose two categories on your review and practice writing objective comments that adhere to the guidelines: clear, specific, business-focused, and self-esteem focused.

5. **Write behavior examples for one of your categories within all levels of performance.**

Where to Go From Here
Helpful Training Topics

- ❑ Goal setting
- ❑ Performance reviews
- ❑ Communication

NINE

TURBULENCE AHEAD...
Navigating Challenging Situations

Chapter Learning Points
- Use experience for challenging situations
- Take action when coaching isn't enough

> *"A coach is someone who can give correction without causing resentment."*
>
> ~John Wooden, basketball coach

Experience Matters

You're on a plane in the middle of a flight, and you hear this announcement: "Ladies and gentlemen, the captain has turned on the fasten seat belt sign. Please return to your seats and keep your seat belts fastened. Thank you." From this statement, you know the pilot is expecting turbulence ahead. A pilot's job is a challenging one even when flying is smooth, and we expect a certain amount of turbulence on just about every flight. When the unusual happens, that is when experience truly matters. Do you remember in 2009 when Captain Chesley "Sully" Sullenberger made an emergency landing in the Hudson River? He safely landed a US Airways flight after the plane hit a flock of geese, damaging both engines and causing the plane to lose power. Makes having a difficult people situation at work seem tame in comparison doesn't it?

Experience matters for pilots as well as managers because you rely not only on your training but on what actually worked and didn't work in prior situations. Challenging people situations are where experienced managers shine and where you can truly be a role model, showing how to interact with others. Experienced managers are more confident in their skills and therefore are more courageous about taking charge of a situation and not paying the price of delay.

Challenging People Situations

You've hired the best person for the job, established an effective performance management process, and created an environment where employees can feel satisfied and engaged. However, there may be situations when a team member's behavior impacts his or her performance and the success of the team in meeting its goals.

The good news is your team members don't get up in the morning thinking: "I wonder how I can make it difficult for my manager today?" or "I think I'll make a mistake on a customer's account today," or "Wouldn't it be fun to violate a policy and see if anyone notices?" So we need to begin by always giving people the benefit of the doubt. Giving someone the benefit of the doubt is when you suspend judgment until you hear all the facts.

If you feel like you are jumping to conclusions, step back and remind yourself to investigate first and ask the question "What else could be happening in this situation?"

Our employees have lives outside of work where they might be experiencing very stressful situations that impact their behavior. They might be worried about a teenager who was experimenting with alcohol, an elderly parent who is showing the first signs of dementia, or a spouse who is despondent about being out of work. Many employees are private and reluctant to about talking about their personal problems. You may only become aware something is wrong by the changes of behavior at work. Giving people the benefit of the doubt recognizes that our employees might have other things going on in their lives that might be spilling over at work.

The saying "perception is reality" means that you leave an impression with people by interacting with them and this causes them to make judgments about your character or abilities. These judgments will sometimes lead to labeling of people.

Experienced managers know the importance of not labeling their team members. Labels tend to stick. Of course we don't mind positive labels like go-getter, creative, efficient, and knowledgeable. But negatively labeling people as difficult, or emotional, or uncooperative impacts your perception of them and how you interact with them. If team members become Carl the Complainer, Cathy the Crier, or David the Difficult, it creates a self-fulfilling prophecy where you start treating the person based on this label. Sometimes, the label causes the team member to behave this way continuously as if it is expected. Mentioning this label to other managers or coworkers also colors their view of the team member, creating a snowball effect and setting up the employee for continued failure. These labels may follow the team member throughout their career with the company.

Every manager recognizes the need to provide feedback and coaching when team members do not perform or behave to specifications. Experienced managers use the feedback process one step sooner by taking the initiative to provide feedback before team members are negatively labeled. This is the "stop it before it sticks" approach. The city's road department uses this approach when it pretreats the bridges and overpasses when they know snow is predicated rather than waiting for accidents to occur while it's snowing.

Of course this feedback might be more difficult when you can't point to less-than-satisfactory performance... yet. But you know if you don't confront the situation now you might be having a disciplinary discussion in the future.

> *"You will never change what you don't confront."*
>
> ~Phumi Ngwane, business consultant

When faced with a challenging employee situation, where there is a possibility of a negative label, take a step back and reflect on answers to these questions:

1. **What specifically is the team member doing?** If you are going to give feedback, you need to be able to describe the behavior with examples. The description should be about observable behavior and not judgments or conclusions about the behavior. Ask yourself, "What exactly did I see or hear?"

2. **Does the behavior matter?** If the behavior doesn't really matter, don't discuss it, but if it does, describe the long-term impact to you, the organization, and the employee.

3. **What can you do to support a change in behavior?** Develop ideas but remember the team member will be more committed to the solution they develop themselves instead of a solution imposed.

Here is an example of this three-step process applied to a specific situation.

1. You have noticed during the last three team meetings that June has been doing most of the talking to the point she has interrupted Julie and Judy several times. You've noticed other team members have been quiet lately and wonder if it's because June "held the floor" for many of the discussions.

2. June has excellent suggestions, but you're concerned that she is inhibiting her team members from contributing their ideas. No one likes to be interrupted, and you have a concern that her team members will perceive June as rude, domineering, and not a team player. You want to avoid her becoming "labeled" with any of these descriptions.

3. Experienced managers know there are two goals in giving feedback: solve the problem and preserve the relationship. You want to make sure June doesn't become defensive and completely stop giving ideas, but you also want her to listen and support ideas given by others. As you plan for the discussion, you make a note to ask June her solutions to solve this perception problem. You also jot down a list of listening tips and probing skills she can use during meetings to include everyone in discussions.

By applying this three-step feedback to challenging people situations early on, you are avoiding the price you'll pay for delaying discussing the situation and prevent the employee from acquiring a negative behavior label.

> *"In the minds of great managers, consistent poor performance is not primarily a matter of weakness, stupidity, disobedience, or disrespect. It is a matter of miscasting."*
>
> ~Marcus Buckingham, author and consultant

When Coaching and Feedback Haven't Worked

If coaching and feedback haven't corrected the situation, it may be time to move to another step in managing performance. Your company will have policies and procedures in place to handle this type of situation. Whether your company refers to it as a performance improvement plan (PIP) or progressive discipline, it is important to know, understand, and comply with the guidelines, including any forms that you need to use and approvals required before undertaking corrective coaching. You may wish to gather the procedure guides and forms your company requires before reading the rest of this chapter.

> *"Executives owe it to the organization and to their fellow workers not to tolerate nonperforming individuals in important jobs."*
>
> ~Peter Drucker, management consultant

Do you see disciplinary discussions as punishment or as a form of coaching and teaching? Many managers avoid beginning their company's corrective process because they view discipline as punishment. Since part of the role of manager is to raise performance levels, discipline is an important part of a manager's job.

When procrastination kicks in, ask yourself: "What is the price of delay?" "Hoping, wishing and praying" that a team member's problem performance or behavior will improve usually doesn't work. The consequence of delaying the disciplinary discussion may include decreased productivity, customer complaints, and low morale from other team members who see nothing being done to correct the problem.

Many organizations follow a practice called progressive discipline, which includes all or some of the following: verbal/oral warning, written warning, final warning, suspension, and discharge. Since suspension is punitive involving docking of pay, it is not used very frequently in today's workplace.

Administering your company's corrective process requires all three C's—competence, confidence, and courage—plus two more related to care:

- **Competence** – to hold the discussion in a professional, problem-solving manner according to your company's policy.

- **Confidence** – that discussing the situation and involving the team member in problem solving will provide the best solution.

- **Courage** – to not procrastinate and pay the price of delay, making the situation worse.

- **Caring** – and showing empathy for the employee who is having difficulty meeting your performance and/or behavior standards.

- Being **careful** – that you don't violate employment laws during your discussion, creating a possible legal liability for your company.

> *"On Discipline: This is a difficult thing to do, to sit down with another person and talk about the fact that they are not doing a good job. And when you have to keep on working with that person, the stakes go up."*
>
> ~Dick Grote, author

The purpose of discipline is to encourage team members to meet established standards of job performance and/or to behave according to established policies and procedures. The root word of discipline means "to teach." By focusing on "teaching" and "helping your employee be the best they can be," the corrective process can be positive, and you can show caring and empathy.

Managers will want to avoid creating an atmosphere of negative discipline focused on punishment, which is inappropriate in a business environment and for today's workforce. When negative discipline is administered, it is done in a harsh or parental sounding tone of voice and quite often focused on the person and their personality instead of objective performance.

Discipline can be positive when it focuses on behavior and not on the person. It offers the employee a chance to participate in discussions and solve problems. Positive discipline is established through good leadership.

The best type of discipline is self-discipline. Self-discipline starts by providing your employees with your performance and on-the-job behavior expectations. While conducting a problem-solving session, your role as a manager is to point out issues of behavior or performance that are substandard. The employee should be viewed as a partner and participate in developing the solution. This action creates an expectation of self-discipline by holding employees accountable. Avoid setting up a situation where the employee feels like a victim and where discipline is something that the manager does to them.

Keep in mind that your decision to implement disciplinary action and possibly even terminate employment, if the situation continues, may be reviewed by a number of outside parties such as the Equal Employment Opportunity Commission (EEOC), the Department of Labor, attorneys, judges, and juries. It is critical that you know, as well as follow, the proscribed corrective process in your organization and develop a good working relationship with your human resources and legal departments.

Before taking action, consider how the situation may appear from outside your organization:

1. **Reasonableness of Rules** – Do the rules and the reasons behind the rules make sense?

2. **Communication and Understanding of Rules** – Have the rules and what violations can lead to disciplinary action been clearly communicated?

3. **Consistency in Applying Discipline** – The disciplinary action should not be arbitrary, inconsistent in application, or illegally discriminatory.

4. **Proof of Violation** – The more in-depth your investigation, the more data and proof you will have that the employee actually committed the offense that requires discipline.

Investigate Before Acting

Part of giving the employee the benefit of the doubt is to conduct an investigation before beginning the disciplinary process. Here are a few questions to ask yourself or others when conducting the investigation:

1. Did the employee know that violating the standard, policy, or rule would result in disciplinary action? Was the standard, policy, or rule in writing?

2. What is the employee's work record? Has the employee received coaching or discipline in the past?

3. What evidence points to the fact the employee was truly the person who committed the wrongdoing? Were witnesses to the incident interviewed?

4. What is the impact to the company, its employees, and customers? How pervasive is the situation, and how often has it happened?

5. Are there extenuating circumstances, such as involvement by another employee, prior instances, or a company practice that may have contributed to the problem?

6. How have similar infractions been dealt with in the past?

Taking this problem solving approach will reduce the tendency to judge the situation too quickly, resulting in the possibility of taking inappropriate disciplinary action.

Discussion Tips

Once you have reviewed your company's policies, procedures, and forms and you have conducted a thorough investigation, it is time to have a discussion with the team member. The discussion can still be held as a problem-solving dialog even though the situation has progressed to the point of corrective action. Here are a few steps to consider:

Step 1: Provide the Facts. After investigating the facts and results of the situation, managers are now ready to share those with the team member. Compare how the observed behavior of the team member differs from expectations established on documents such as job descriptions, company policies, and/or procedure manuals. Any previous coaching discussions should also be mentioned during Step 1.

Example: *Sheldon, as you know quality is a key competency for your position. I'd like to show you three reports you've completed during the past two weeks that contain errors. I noticed one of these errors before it went out to the customer, and you and I were able to correct it. Unfortunately, the other customers received the other two reports with errors.*

Step 2: Probe and Listen. It is now your turn to listen. Ask probing questions to determine the team member's point of view on the situation and possible barriers to acceptable performance. Managers should apply active listening skills to encourage the employee to participate in the discussion to identify barriers and solutions. Keep an open mind during this part of the problem-solving session and not rush to your own conclusion.

Example: *I would like us to spend time on a problem-solving session concerning this situation. What do you think is causing these errors? Is there something happening that I should know about? What solutions do you have for preventing future errors?*

Step 3: Discuss Process. This is the time to discuss your company's form and disciplinary process, keeping in mind that some organizations refer to this process as a performance improvement plan.

Example: *Sheldon, thank you for participating in our problem-solving discussion today. We agreed on the following plan to avoid further errors in the future. On Wednesday you will sit with Frank to learn a few of his quantity and quality techniques. You also agreed to conduct a final check on your work before sending reports out to customers. Finally, we agreed that you will let me know if you feel so rushed you become concerned about making an error. Our discussion today will be documented per our company's policies and procedures.*

Step 4: Create Required Documentation. By documenting your conversation on your company's required form and obtaining approval signatures if necessary, you will be able to accurately recall the details of the discussion if possible future disciplinary discussions, including termination of employment, becomes necessary if the problem isn't corrected.

> *"It's not the people you fire who make your life miserable. It's the people you don't."*
>
> ~Dick Grote, author *Discipline Without Punishment*

Strategies for Difficult Discipline Situations

Despite all your research and preplanning for the disciplinary discussion, situations may arise that will present a challenge. It is impossible to be able to totally predict the reaction of others; however, an experienced manager prepares for every possibility.

As part of your preplanning for the discussion, you will think of an employee's possible barriers to successful performance and reactions the employee may exhibit. Studying the following strategies and planning your responses now will give you more confidence in handling challenging discussion situations when they actually occur. As you read each strategy, think about the types of situations where it would apply.

1. **Referral to the Employee Assistance Program (EAP).** If your organization offers an EAP, it will provide personal counseling for employees and their family. Managers are not in a position to offer counseling of a personal nature, which should always be conducted by a trained professional. By referring employees to the EAP to discuss and help resolve your employee's personal issues, you can then remain focused on the business issues.

2. **Conduct the Discussion in Two Sessions.** Occasionally the employee is not emotionally prepared to participate in an effective problem-solving session. This reaction could be due to the employee being surprised by the problem or he or she being someone who typically exhibits a strong emotional response to corrective action discussions. If you feel a more productive, problem-solving session could be held if delayed, set a date and time as soon as possible, indicating to the employee the need to be prepared to discuss the issues and solutions at that time.

3. **Request a Coaching or a Practice Session.** If you anticipate the disciplinary session will be challenging or that issues may be discussed that will make you

feel concerned, use the expertise of your manager or the human resources department for coaching tips. Your company policy may state that another manager or member of human resources is required to attend your discussion with the team member.

The disciplinary process is more effective and less stressful for you and your team members when discipline is seen as another problem to be solved while you engage the team members as equals in solving the problem. Begin today with a new viewpoint of discipline, and you will see raised performance in your organization.

Summary

Experienced managers don't wait for a behavior problem to become severe; they are proactive with their coaching to avoid negatively labeling team members. When behavior or performance problems continue after coaching and feedback, experienced managers begin their company's disciplinary process, sometimes called performance improvement plans. The five C's that are used in discipline are confidence, competence, courage, caring, and careful.

Building Your Map
Follow-up Activities

1. **Brainstorm several negative labels you have heard to describe a team member.** Think about the consequences these labels had on employees and their careers. Provide an example.

2. **Reflect on the behavior of your team members.** Are any in danger of being negatively labeled? If yes, plan a discussion based on these reflective questions: What specifically is the team member doing? Does the behavior matter? What can you do to support a change in behavior?

3. **Collect information about your company's policies, procedures, and forms related to corrective performance situations.**

4. **Plan a disciplinary discussion for a situation that might become necessary in the future using:** Step 1: Provide the facts. Step 2: Probe and listen. Step 3: Discuss process. Step 4: Create required documentation.

5. **Locate information on your organization's employee assistance program if applicable.**

Where to Go From Here
Helpful Training Topics

❑ Coaching and feedback
❑ Disciplinary action
❑ Communication and listening skills

TEN

RECALCULATING...
Continuous Improvement on Your Management Journey

Chapter Learning Points
- Create a continuous improvement culture
- Apply the spirit of continuous improvement to your management journey

> *"If you're any good at all, you know you can be better."*
>
> ~Lindsey Buckingham, musician

> *"He who stops being better, stops being good."*
>
> ~Oliver Cromwell, English political leader

Continuous Improvement for Your Team

The Olympic motto is made up of three Latin words: *citius, altius, fortius*. These words mean faster, higher, stronger. The motto is meant to inspire athletes to embrace the Olympic spirit, perform to the best of their abilities, and strive for improvement.

Managers can capture the Olympic spirit for their department, to inspire their team members to always strive to perform at the best of their abilities. What type of manager fosters this spirit in the workplace?

- They are the type of manager who always looks for ways to improve their team's quality of work.
- They encourage their team to seek opportunities to improve general work processes, methods, and systems.
- They empower their team members to make suggestions for improvement and just not to just accept the status quo.
- They are willing to alter current processes and methods when appropriate if it benefits the customer and makes the workplace more productive.

In the business world, the Olympic spirit is known as continuous improvement. It involves employees in searching for and eliminating wasteful, unproductive processes and improving quality. As an experienced manager it is important to know and follow your company's process. Your program might be known as Total Quality Management, Lean Manufacturing, Six Sigma, or Kaizen—a Japanese term meaning "improvement" or "change for the best."

Some of these quality initiatives require a formal certification process including an exam and successful project completion. They each take a slightly different approach, but what they have in common is they get employees involved with their work and with fellow team members to improve processes, productivity, quality, and safety. Employees are encouraged to come up with small improvement suggestions on a regular basis. These suggestions are not a once a month or once a year activity, they are continuous.

All formal continuous improvement programs utilize some form of tools and techniques. Here are a few ideas you can immediately start using with your team members that don't have a financial cost to implement: Plus/Delta, Process Flow Analysis, and Work Out.

Plus/Delta

The Plus/Delta method is a quick, easy-to-use activity that can be conducted after every project or business cycle to provide ideas for continuous improvement. It is a "lessons learned" activity and a means of identifying what is going well and what needs to be changed. The "Plus" represents the pluses of how the team performed and what should be repeated in the future; it's an opportunity to celebrate successes and gain satisfaction about what worked. The "Delta," which is a letter in the Greek alphabet basically meaning change, represents things that didn't go quite as well and should be modified or stopped in the future. The Delta items, those things that didn't quite work this time, should be written as action-oriented solutions for the future.

Teams have a couple ways to perform this activity, including having team members each make their own list on separate pieces of paper or using flip chart paper in a group brainstorming session. The "T" shape drawn on the chart typically has a "+" on one side and a "Δ" on the other. Yet another method is to give two colors of self-stick notes to your team members. They use one color to note the things that went well for the Plus side, and the other color represents the Delta ideas—the action items.

Plus/Delta can become a regular part of your team meetings where you generally talk about performance during the last week/month or after a specific project. It can even be used during individual performance review discussions. You will know the process is working when your team members suggest a Plus/Delta session on their own!

> **"Quality is doing the right thing when no one is looking."**
>
> ~Henry Ford, founder Ford Motor Company

Process Flow Analysis

If you want your team members to analyze methods and processes, it is important to teach them to use quality analysis tools. Process Flow Analysis is one of the simplest and most effective tools you can teach your team members.

It's amazing how many processes get changed over the years. They get changed when different individuals create their own steps to get things done and then hand down those steps via one-on-one training to others. The process turns into something that resembles a patchwork quilt, similar to a road with filled potholes. Sometimes important steps are left out and other unnecessary steps are added. As a manager, you might not even be aware of what has been changed.

A Process Flow Analysis visually documents each step involved in a procedure or process. By conducting this analysis you are likely to 1) uncover bottlenecks in the process, 2) determine how many people "touch" the process, and 3) if you add a length of time to complete along with each step, you can determine the total time needed to complete each process.

An easy way to complete this analysis is to set up a flip chart stand with paper and gather everyone involved in the process. Ask the question, "What is the first thing that happens?" Then write that step at the top of the chart followed by a down arrow. Then keep asking the group "what happens next" and write down each step in succession. You might be surprised at the disagreements about what happens next, and then you will uncover the extra steps some team members are doing, that there are overlapping responsibilities, or find gaps in the process. Adding the people involved in the step and the length of time it takes to complete each step to your chart will provide even more data.

After completing the analysis, determine if any steps can be added or eliminated to improve efficiency or to improve quality. The end result can become a pictorial work chart or standard operating procedure. With enough practice, team members will be able to complete this process alone or with other team members in the spirit of continuous improvement.

Work-Out

When I was with GE Capital, the financial services company of General Electric, we participated in a terrific process called Work-Out. Work-Out became a successful process for challenging bureaucracy, eliminating duplicate effort, and taking the unnecessary work out.

> *"Trust the people in the organization—the people in the best position to improve a business are the people in the job every day."*
>
> ~Jack Welch, former GE CEO

Work-Out is a structured way to quickly solicit ideas for work reduction and for those ideas to be implemented as soon as possible. Your team members might be thinking "there must be a better way" right now, but lack the opportunity to present their ideas in a productive way. Work-Out provides the formalized process for all employees to be able to question the status quo and the assumption of "that's the way we've always done it."

A Work-Out session is planned and facilitated with specific goals in mind. Example: "We need to stop spending time on duplicate or unnecessary reports." Teams can request advice from technical experts in other departments such as information technology, finance, or human resources. The most powerful part of Work-Out compared to other employee involvement initiatives is the commitment by the decision maker to make an on-the-spot yes or no decision based on the recommendations. If the answer is yes, the participants are empowered to develop and implement an action plan for their suggestion.

Examples of Work-Out improvements include reduced cycle time, streamlined processes, and elimination of redundant reports. For more in-depth information on how to implement Work-Out in your organization, refer to book *The GE Work-Out*, referenced in the bibliography at the back of this book.

Creating a Culture of Continuous Improvement

> *"Quality is free. It's not a gift, but it's free. The 'unquality' things are what cost money."*
>
> ~Philip B. Crosby, author *Quality Is Free*

Managers are in a unique position to impact and reinforce the culture within their departments. They can create a culture of continuous improvement by implementing practices that encourage all team members to "think quality improvement" until it becomes second nature. Following are a few best practices. As you read each one, think about what you already do and which items you would like to implement in your department.

• Create the expectation that every team member is required to be constantly growing, learning, and contributing to the overall goal.
• Allow room for team members to experiment. If team members say "I have an idea," let them try it.
• When you learn something new about the company or a new skill, share it with your team.

- Create a "no blame" environment for team members to bring up problems on the job.
- Allow time for team members to attend training.
- Reward and recognize team members who develop suggestions for improvement.

Self-Development

We've been exploring continuous improvement for your team members. Now it's time to discuss your continuous improvement as a manager. Managers who embrace a mindset of continuous improvement embrace a principal of self-reflection. Self-reflection can be conducted in three steps.

Step I: Think about activities or projects where you have really excelled. Now reflect on the type of skills you used. Is there a pattern? When we have the opportunity to use our natural skills, we feel energized, willing and able to focus our attention for however long it takes to get it done. We feel a sense of accomplishment at the end.

Step II: Think about activities or projects that haven't gone so well. Reflect on the type of skills you had to use. Is there a pattern here? When we have to use skills that are not our natural strengths, we tend to feel drained of energy and quite often procrastinate in completing our activities or projects. We have a sense of "thank goodness that's over" at the end.

Step III: Go back to the strengths you identified in Step I and reflect if these strengths are going to serve you or obstruct you in your next career opportunity. You may have to tone down your strengths so they don't become weaknesses. Obtain information on what strengths are valuable for the future position you identified.

Step IV: Go back to the skills you identified as not your natural strengths in Step II. Will you need to use more or less of these skills if you advance to your next opportunity? If you'll use them less...great! If you'll need to use them more, it may be time to either start building these skills or re-evaluate if the next opportunity is truly the best fit for you.

Sometimes during your reflection you realize you might have to get off the road you are on and "recalculate" your management map route. Here are a couple of examples of the result of self-reflection:

Gene is an accountant; he holds an advanced degree in accounting and keeps current in his field. He excels and enjoys the detailed work of accounting but lately finds it a bit isolating. He begins to reflect about "what's next" and realizes what energizes him is interacting with people and sharing his accounting knowledge through teaching. He decides to go back to school to obtain his Ph.D. and teach at the university level.

Angela is a professional training consultant. She is an engaging facilitator and receives excellent reviews for her stand-up training delivery. When Angela reflects on what energizes her and what drains her energy, she realizes what she enjoys the most is the development of quality training programs instead of the delivery. She decides to use her analytical and project management skills to design training programs and begins a self-study of current software to assist her.

Emily reflects that if she is to move to the next level in her career, she needs to develop her managerial skills. Emily excels as an individual contributor but hasn't had much practice in leading other people. Even though interaction with people sometimes drains her energy, she accepts a lateral move that lets her supervise others and build her skills. She also attends training classes, reads books on leadership, and has volunteered as a leader in her professional association. Emily may come to enjoy managing others or may go back to an individual-contributor role, but she is keeping an open mind during the experience.

> *"I think it's very important to have a feedback loop, where you're constantly thinking about what you've done and how you could be doing it better. I think that's the single best piece of advice: constantly think about how you could be doing things better and questioning yourself."*
>
> ~Elon Musk, founder of Tesla Motors and Space Exploration Technologies

Feedback on Your Management Style

In addition to self-reflection, experienced managers seek feedback from others about their leadership behavior for continuous improvement.

One of the best ways to get feedback is through a 360 review process, in which managers receive confidential, anonymous feedback from the people who work around them. This process typically includes their manager, peers, and direct reports. Because you are getting the perspective of all the people who interact with you on a regular basis from different points of view, it is like looking at your management map from the north, south, east, and west. What a great way to really learn how your behavior impacts others!

> *"We all need people who will give us feedback. That's how we improve."*
>
> ~Bill Gates, founder of Microsoft, philanthropist

Some managers avoid using a 360 feedback process and feel defensive about the results. Experienced managers recognize their thoughts and feelings around this process and then proceed anyway because of how valuable the information will be in their career. They need to know there are skills for them to develop before they become so ingrained it's difficult to change their behavior.

When you get your feedback, look at the results and compare it to your vision of how you want to be as a manager. You will find you will be pleased with your feedback in some areas but might need to make changes in other areas.

The management team of Olivia, Ethan, and Madelyn decide to use a 360 review to improve their management practices. Consider these examples:

- **Example I:** Olivia finds out she has the reputation of being someone who can get things done, which fits with her self-image as a manager. She also receives feedback that she sometimes communicates in an abrupt manner when people don't understand concepts as easily as she does. Olivia now knows she should work more on her patience and interpersonal skills.

- **Example II:** Ethan sees himself as an enthusiastic team builder and his 360 feedback confirms that others see this in his management style as well. His team members always appear to be enjoying their work. His development identified was to improve follow-up on projects and to meet deadlines. He will attend project management and time management training classes.

- **Example III:** Madelyn is a risk taker and embodies the characteristic of courage. She regularly seeks out challenging assignments for herself and her team. She has always been adventurous at work and in her personal life, hiking and scuba diving. You name it and Madelyn has tried it. Her team members, however, provide feedback within her 360 that they sometimes feel exhausted by the constant new challenges and want more stability in their environment. Madelyn decides she needs to communicate and listen more to her team to learn more about their workload before committing to new projects.

The raters in your process will appreciate a follow up. Your follow up can be in the form of saying thank you, inviting further feedback by asking questions, and discussing your action plans. End by asking for their support as you make changes.

> *"I think it's become an economic necessity for people to be able to learn and grow throughout their lives, because most people can't get through their entire career with one skill set. We have to keep reinventing ourselves."*
>
> ~Chesley Sullenberger, retired airline pilot

Summary

All people have the opportunity for continuous improvement throughout their careers. Experienced managers can create a spirit and culture of continuous improvement by encouraging and expecting suggestions from all team members and implementing quality initiatives. Managers themselves can model the way for continuous improvement by using self-reflection and asking for feedback from others.

Building Your Map
Follow-up Activities

1. **Determine if your company has a quality or continuous improvement initiative.** What is it called? Who is in charge of the initiative? What tools or processes are available to teach your team?

2. **Facilitate a Plus/Delta session at your next team meeting.** First, teach your team the purpose of the Plus/Delta and the ground rules that the Deltas, changes for the future, need to be expressed as action plans.

3. **Train your team members on the use of a quality tool.** Consider Process Flow Analysis or any other quality tools available through your company.

4. **Perform a Self-Reflection activity.**
   - **Step I:** The skills used during successful activities/projects.
   - **Step II:** Skills used during less-than-successful activities/projects.
   - **Step III:** Are your strengths identified going to serve you or obstruct you in your next career opportunity?
   - **Step IV:** Will you need to use more or less of these skills identified in Step II?

5. **Request a 360 review. Ask your company if it offers a 360 review process.** Go through the process and develop an action plan, including providing that plan to your raters.

Where to Go From Here
Helpful Training Topics

- ☐ Problem solving
- ☐ Facilitation skills
- ☐ Quality/Continuous Improvement training
- ☐ 360 review

EPILOGUE

ARE WE THERE YET?

> *"Every new beginning comes from some other beginning's end."*
>
> ~Seneca, Roman philosopher

Children everywhere seem to ask the same question, "Are we there yet?" It means I'm bored on this journey and am anxious to arrive at our destination. You might also be familiar with the question "When are we leaving?" Having decided that they are bored with the destination, your children are ready to move on to somewhere new.

Experienced managers have learned that it's also about the management journey, not necessarily only about the destination. We know the importance of goal setting and the feeling of accomplishment when we're successful; however, there is also satisfaction in staying present and reflecting on what we are experiencing and learning along the way.

Remember Judy, the manager we met in Chapter 1? She has just accepted a new job. The position is a managerial position in the global division in her company, and she will manage people not only in the

U.S. but also in France. She is of course excited about the opportunity to use her French language skills and to take on a new challenge. Her new team is much larger and she will have three supervisors reporting to her to assist in managing the department. The change will mark an ending to her current role and launch the beginning of a new journey with new discoveries.

Judy realizes that she will be able to grow her management map and reflects on the following questions as she prepares to take on her new responsibility:

- ❑ What have I learned as an experienced manager that I can take to my new job?
- ❑ How will managing people in another country differ from managing people in the U.S.?
- ❑ How will I get to know my new team members?
- ❑ How will I mentor the three supervisors so they too can develop their management maps?
- ❑ What expectations do I have for the new role and how will I communicate them?
- ❑ What do I want to learn in my new role?

I know that Judy will be successful in her new role since she is a fully engaged employee and a lifelong learner.

Has this book inspired you to add to your management map? Where will your management journey take you next?

- ❑ **On the Road Again**, using experienced manager skills and transitioning to leadership?
- ❑ Expanding your map to **Navigate Globally**?

- ❑ Getting **An Arial View** of your corporate culture?
- ❑ Getting top talent **All Aboard**?
- ❑ Creating a strong team by getting **All Hands on Deck**?
- ❑ Building the engagement of your team for **Commitment to the Journey**?
- ❑ Holding career planning conversations by **Creating a Map for Your Team?**
- ❑ Managing performance on **The Road to Excellence**?
- ❑ **Experiencing Turbulence Ahead** when navigating challenging situations?
- ❑ **Recalculating** through continuous improvement?

I believe that every manager has the ability to become a great manager, wherever your particular management journey takes you. Great managers enjoy their journey and also help everyone else they connect with to "be the best they can be." Enjoy your management journey.

"We are at our very best, and we are the happiest, when we are fully engaged in work we enjoy on the journey toward the goal we've established for ourselves. It gives meaning to our time off and comfort to our sleep. It makes everything else in life so wonderful, so worthwhile."

~Earl Nightingale, American radio personality

BIBLIOGRAPHY

Bolles, Richard N. *What Color Is Your Parachute? 2015: A Practical Manual for Job-Hunters and Career-Changers.* New York, NY: Crown Publishing Group, 2014.

Buckingham, Marcus and Curt Coffman. *First Break All the Rules: What the World's Greatest Managers Do Differently.* New York, NY: Simon & Schuster, 1999.

Collins, James C. *Good to Great: Why Some Companies Make the Leap and Others Don't.* New York, NY: Harper Business, 2001.

Goldsmith, Marshall. *What Got You Here Won't Get You There.* New York, NY: Hyperion, 2007.

Grote, Dick. *How to Be Good at Performance Appraisals...Simple, Effective, Done Right.* Boston, MA: Harvard Business School Publishing, 2011.

Lencioni, Patrick. *The Five Dysfunctions of a Team: A Leadership Fable.* San Francisco, CA: Jossey-Bass, 2002.

Lencioni, Patrick. *The Three Signs of a Miserable Job: A Fable for Managers.* San Francisco, CA: Jossey-Bass, 2007.

Rath, Tom. *Now, Discover Your Strengths.* New York, NY: Gallup Press, 2007.

Stamm, Susan. *42 Rules of Employee Engagement (2nd Edition): A Straightforward Look at What It Takes to Build a Culture of Engagement.* Cupertino, CA: Superstar Press, 2012.

Straw, Julie, Barry Davis, Mark Scullard, Susie Kukkonen. *The Work of Leaders...How Vision, Alignment, and Execution Will Change the Way You Lead.* San Francisco, CA: John Wiley and Sons, 2013.

Ulrich, Dave, Steve Kerr, Ron Ashkenas. *The GE Work-Out: How to Implement GE's Revolutionary Method for Busting Bureaucracy & Attacking Organizational Problems—Fast!* New York, NY: McGraw-Hill, 2002.

Youngberg, Carl. *Make Yourself Matter...Become Your Own Asset.* Dallas, TX: Experts That Speak, 2008.

RESOURCES FOR YOUR MANAGEMENT JOURNEY

Management Skills Resource, Inc. is your resource for all your management development training needs. Our products and services are dedicated to the advancement and on-the-job application of effective management principles.

Building the *competence*, *confidence,* and *courage* of your management teams through:

Classroom Training – Using proven templates, we custom design workshops based on your company's culture, policies, and procedures.

Training Products – Our learning products are always designed to align people's skills and behavior with organizational strategies.

Management Skills Resource, Inc.

www.ManagementSkillsResource.com
Info@ManagementSkillsResource

ABOUT THE AUTHOR

Deborah Avrin, MS, SPHR, brings more than 20 years of human resources and training experience to her company, Management Skills Resource, Inc. Her coaching skills have assisted countless managers to improve their performance in such diverse industries as financial services, manufacturing, utilities, transportation, education, non-profit, and telecommunications.

Prior to beginning her consulting practice in 1998, Deborah held a variety of top-level human resources leadership positions in both the financial services and manufacturing industries. She also has held operational management positions, which enables her to understand the unique training needs of managers. Her reputation is as a motivator, with an inspiring training style that encourages others to excel.

Her company, Management Skills Resource, Inc., works with organizations that want to build the confidence, competence, and courage of their management teams through creative training workshops.

Her educational background includes a BBA in human resources and a masters degree in organizational behavior. Deborah also holds a lifetime Senior Professional in Human Resources (SPHR) certification.

The Management Map II: Navigation Tools for Managers Transitioning to Leadership is the second in the Management Map series.

www.ingramcontent.com/pod-product-compliance
Lightning Source LLC
Chambersburg PA
CBHW060553210326
41519CB00014B/3456